UGC NET : REVISED FORMAT

# Library and Information Science

UGC NET : REVISED FORMAT

# Library and Information Science

Volume II

## CRITIQUE AND DEFINITIONAL QUESTIONS

C.K. Sharma
Akhil Kumar Singh

ATLANTIC
PUBLISHERS & DISTRIBUTORS (P) LTD

Published by

**ATLANTIC**

**PUBLISHERS & DISTRIBUTORS (P) LTD**

B-2, Vishal Enclave, Opp. Rajouri Garden,
New Delhi-110027
Phones : +91-11-25413460, 25429987, 25466842

Sales Office
7/22, Ansari Road, Darya Ganj,
New Delhi-110002
Phones : +91-11-23273880, 23275880, 23280451
Fax : +91-11-23285873
web : www.atlanticbooks.com
e-mail : info@atlanticbooks.com

Chennai Branch
5, Nallathambi Street, Wallajah Road,
Chennai-600002
Phones : +91-44-64611085, 32413319
e-mail : chennai@atlanticbooks.com



Printed in India
at Nice Printing Press, Delhi

# Preface

The University Grants Commission has revised its syllabus of National Eligibility Test (NET) for social and humanity disciplines. This book Library & Information Science in 3 volumes is based on the revised format of UGC NET.

Volume I contains the multiple choice questions (MCQs) of the following type:

(a) Multiple choice—tick the correct option.

(b) Matching type.

(c) True/False.

(d) Assertion-Reason type.

There will be 50 multiple choice questions. Each question will be of 2 marks (Total 100 marks).

Volume II covers Sections I and II of Paper III—which will have 4 sections.

Section I requires a candidate to write a critique of a given passage from a known thinker/writer or of a stanza from some poem of an established poet. There will be five questions asked from a given passage requiring an answer based on the contents and inferences of the passage. This Section shall carry 5 × 5 = 25 marks.

Section II requires a candidate to answer 15 questions asked across the syllabus for Paper III (Part A). The questions will be definitional or seeking particular information and are to be answered in about 30 words each. The questions in this Section shall be numbered from 6 to 20, and each question shall carry 5 marks, making a total of 5 × 15 = 75 marks.

Volume III caters to the evaluative and essay type questions asked respectively under Section III and IV of Paper III of UGC-NET revised format. Structured in two sections, the book contains both brief and detailed explanation of terms related to library and information science in an alphabetical order.

In the combined form, all the three Volumes constitute an ideal book on library and information science for the aspirants of NET. It will not only enhance their knowledge of the subject but will also help them revise the known facts in a quick manner. I wish all my readers a great success in National Eligibility Test (NET).

I am very much thankful to Dr. K.R. Gupta, Chairman of Atlantic Publishers and Distributors (P) Ltd., New Delhi who found this book worth publishing.

**C.K. SHARMA**

# Contents

## VOLUME I



## VOLUME II



## VOLUME III

## Section-I

# Critique

# PAPER III

**Passage-1 (UGC Samples Passage)**

**Read the following passage and answer the questions:**

The Constitution guarantees every citizen the fundamental right to equality. Yet after about 60 years of independence, just one perusal of the female infant mortality figures, the literacy rates and the employment opportunities for women is sufficient evidence that discrimination exists. Almost predictably, this gender bias is evident in our political system as well. In the 13th Lok Sabha, there were 43 women MPs out of a total of 543; it is not a surprising figure, for never has women's representation in Parliament been more than 10 per cent.

Historically, the manifestos of major political parties have always encouraged women's participation. It has been merely a charade. So, women's organizations, denied a place on merit, opted for the last resort: a reservation of seats for women in Parliament and State Assemblies. Parties, which look at everything with a vote bank in mind, seemed to endorse this. Alas, this too was a mirage.

But there is another aspect also. At a time when caste is the trump card, some politicians want the bill to include further quotas for women from among minorities and backward castes. There is more to it. A survey shows that there is a general antipathy towards the bill. It is actually a classic case of doublespeak—in public, politicians were endorsing women's reservation but in the backrooms of Parliament, they were busy sabotaging it. The reasons are clear: Men just don't want to vacate their seats of power.

Q. 1. The problem raised in the passage reflects badly on our:

(a) Political system

(b) Social behaviour

(c) Individual behaviour

(d) Behaviour of a group of people

Q. 2 According to the passage, political parties have mostly in mind:

(a) Economic prosperity

(b) Vote bank

(c) People's welfare

(d) Patriotism

Q. 3 "Trump Card" means:

(a) Trying to move a dead horse

(b) Playing the card cautiously

(c) Sabotaging all the moves by others

(d) Making the final jolt for success

Q. 4. The sentence "Men just don't want to vacate their seats of power" implies:

a) Lust for power

(b) Desire to serve the nation

(c) Conviction in one's own political abilities

(d) Political corruption

Q. 5. What is the percentage of women in the Lok Sabha:

(a) 10 (b) 7.91 (c) 43 (d) 9.1

**Passage-2**

**Read the following passage and answer the questions:**

The test of a great book is whether we want to read it only once or more than once. Any really great book is that which we want to read the second time even more than we wanted to read it the first time, and every additional time that we read it we find new meanings and new beauties in it. A book that a person of education and good taste does not care to read more than once is very probably not worth much. But we cannot consider the judgment of a single individual infallible. The opinion that makes a book great must be the opinion of many. For even the greatest critics are apt to have certain dullness, certain inappreciations. Carlyle, for example, could not endure Browning. Byron could not endure some of the greatest English poets. A man must be many-sided to utter a trustworthy estimate of many books. We may doubt the judgment of the single critic at times. But there is no doubt possible in regard to the judgment of generations. Even if we cannot at once perceive anything good in a book which has been admired and praised for hundreds of years, we may be sure that by trying, by studying it carefully, we shall at last be able to feel the reason of this admiration and praise. The best of all libraries for a poor man would be a library composed of such great works only, books which have passed the test of time.

*–Lafcadio Hearn*

Q. 1. The test of great book is:

(a) It is read once and gives satisfaction

(b) It is read again and again and then satisfies us

(c) It is read second time and even more, and every additional time it gives new meaning and beauties

Q. 2. The book can be judged by:

(a) Single reader

(b) Single critic

(c) One time reader

(d) Single individual infallible

(e) Judgment of generations

Q. 3. Carlyle could not endure:

(a) Byron (b) Hardy

(c) Carlyle (d) Browning

Q. 4. Libraries composed of great works only, are the best of all libraries which have:

(a) Served the people

(b) Housed maximum number of books

(c) Engaged maximum staff
(d) Passed the test of time

Q. 5. The passage is aimed at finding out:
(a) Who a great critic is
(b) The parameters of judging the quality of a book
(c) The qualities of a good library

**Passage-3**

**Read the following passage and answer the questions:**

A book is essentially not a talked thing, but a written thing; and written, not with the view of mere communication but of permanence. The book of talk is printed only because its author cannot speak to thousands of people at once; if he could, he would—the volume is mere multiplication of his voice. You cannot talk to your friend in India; if you could, you would; you write instead; that is mere conveyance of voice; but a book is written, not to multiply the voice merely but to perpetuate it. The author has something to say which he perceives to be true and useful, or helpfully beautiful. So far as he knows, no one has yet said it; so far as he knows, no one else can say it. He is bound to say it clearly and melodiously if he may; clearly, at all events. In the sum of his life he finds this to be the thing, or group of things, manifest to him; this, the piece of true knowledge, or sight, which his share of sunshine and earth has permitted him to seize. He would set it down for ever; engrave it on rock, if he could; saying, "This is the best of me; for the rest, I ate and drank, and slept, loved and hated, like another; my life was as the vapour, and is no more; but this I saw and knew; this, if anything of mine, is worth your memory". That is his 'writing'; it is in his small human way, and with whatever degree of true inspiration is in him, his inscription, or scripture. That is a book.

Q. 1. Book is essentially a:
(a) Talking thing
(b) Written think
(c) Mere communication
(d) Performance communication

Q. 2. The passage "the book of talk is printed only because its author cannot speak to thousands of people at once" implies:

(a) Conveyance of voice

(b) Written form

(c) Perpetuation of voice

Q. 3. The book is a:

(a) Clarify of events

(b) Manifestation of ideas

(c) Piece of true knowledge

Q. 4. The Books (writings) are worth of:

(a) Memory

(b) What we saw and knew

(c) True inspiration

(d) Inspiration and inscription of a man

Q. 5. A good book normally aims at:

(a) Communication of ideas

(b) Entertainment

(c) Preparation of knowledge, information & inspiration

(d) None of the above

**Passage-4**

**Read the following passage and answer the questions:**

What, then, is the nature of this educational process? How is education, in the sense of the development and culture of the mind, possible? This process of mental culture or real education shows a striking resemblance to the process of the growth and development of the human body. As the body from its embryonic beginnings grows and develops to its full stature by means of suitable assimilable food, movement and exercise in accordance with physical and chemical laws, so does the mind grow and develop from its original dispositions to its full evolutionary cultivation by means of mental food and mental exercise according to the laws of mental growth.

This mental food is supplied to the mind by the cultural goods of the society in which it is placed; its sciences, its arts, its techniques, its religion, its customs, its moral and legal codes, its social forms, its institutions, its personalities. These material and immaterial goods of culture are all of them the product of mental effort of some individuals or groups. There are products or images signifying the meaning their originators sought to embody in them. They are objectifications of the human with a significance, objective external facts with a meaning. In this objective form they carry the impression and portray the structure, vaguely perhaps, at times, but definitely and distinctly at others, of the mind which formed them. The quality of the thought and feeling, of the desire and accomplishment of their creatures has become latent in them. They are, so to say, the storehouse of their mental energy.

Now these cultural goods are the only means of setting the educational process into motion, they are the only food for the cultivation of the human mind. Surrounded by the treasures of culture, which society has placed at its disposal, the growing mind, unconsciously at first, more and more consciously later, takes hold of the cultural goods and uses them for its gradual development. When these goods of culture are so used they become educative goods; cultivated minds had produced them. They, now cultivate other minds.

The important truth to be kept in view in organizing education is that the cultivation of the individual mind by means of cultural goods is possible only when the mental structure wholly or partially corresponds to them. I feel sure in my mind that this basic axiom of the educational process, the axiom of congruence between the individual mind and the mental structure of the cultural goods used for its cultivation will be the guiding principle of our future educational development.

*—Dr. Zakir Hussain*
*(A Broadcast Talk on the A.I.R.)*

Q. 1. The nature of educational process is to develop:

(a) The knowledge (b) The behaviour
(c) The social environment
(d) The culture of mind

Q. 2. Body grows and develops to its full stature by means of:
(a) Food
(b) Movement
(c) Exercise
(d) Assimilable food, movement and exercise

Q. 3. The problem raised in passage is reflecting obviously on our:
(a) Mental food
(b) Cultural goods
(c) Growth of mind
(d) Educational process

Q. 4 Guiding principles of our future educational development are:
(a) Feelings and exercise
(b) Educational process
(c) Mental structure of the cultural goods
(d) Treasure of culture

Q. 5. Individual mental structure and the mentality of the cultural goods are:
(a) Identical
(b) Diametrically opposed
(c) Different but should have congruence

**Passage-5**

**Read the following passage and answer the questions:**

The fact remains that conversation is a real art, and depends, like all other arts, upon congenial circumstances and suitable surrounding. People are too apt to believe that because they have interests in their minds and can put those interests into words, they are equipped for the pretty and delicate game of talk. But a rare admixture of qualities is needed, and a subtle conversational effect, a sudden fancy, that, throws a charming or a bizarre light on a subject, a power of pleasing metaphorical expression, the communication of an imaginative interest to a familiar topic—all these things are of the nature, of instinctive art. I have heard well-informed and sensible people talk of a subject in a way that made me feel that I desired never to hear it mentioned again; but I have heard, on the other hand, people talk of matters which I had believed to be worn threadbare by use, and yet communicate a rich colour, a fragrant sentiment to them, which made me feel that I had never thought adequately on the topic before. On should be careful, I think, to express to such persons one's appreciation and admiration of their gifts, for the art is so rare that we ought to welcome it when we find it; and like all arts, it depends to a great extent for its sustenance on the avowed gratitude of those who enjoy it. It is on these subtle, half-toned glimpses of personality and difference that most of our happy expressions of life depend; and no one can afford willfully to neglect sources of innocent joy, or to lose opportunities of leisure through a stupid or brutal contempt for the slender resources out of which gentle effects are produced.

*–A.C. Benson*

Q. 1. The fact remains that conversation depends on:

(a) Congenial environment
(b) Belief
(c) Events
(d) Congenial circumstances

Q. 2. The man with his interest in mind expresses:

(a) By behaviour
(b) By attitude
(c) By action
(d) By pretty and delicate talks

Q. 3. The sentence "sensitive people talk of a subject in a way that made me feel" means that:

(a) They are not worth hearing
(b) They are not to be considered
(c) They are communicative
(d) They are not desired to hear but still they are heard

Q. 4. 'Conversation is a real art', applied to:
(a) Express one's appreciation
(b) Express one's gratitude
(c) Happiness
(d) Knowledge transfer

Q. 5. The passage suggests whether:
(a) Only gravity of the subject is important
(b) Only conversational skills are important
(c) Gravity of the subject is important but conversational skills are even more important

**Passage-6**

**Read the following passage and answer the questions:**

A public library should contain something for all tastes, as well as the material necessary for a thorough grounding in all branches of knowledge. It should be rich in books of reference, in encyclopaedias, where one may learn without cost of research what things are generally known. For it is far more useful to know these than to know those that are not generally known. Not to know them is the defect of those half-trained and therefore hasty men who find a mare's nest on every branch of the tree of knowledge. A library should contain ample stores of history, which teaches many things profitable for us to know and lay to heart; teaches, among other things, how much of the present is influenced by the past; teaches that, if there be no controlling purpose, there is, at least, a sternly logical sequence in human affairs, and that chance has but a trifling dominion over them, teaches why things are and must be so and not otherwise. I would have plenty of biography. It is no insignificant fact that eminent men have always loved their Plutarch, since example, whether for emulation or avoidance, is never so poignant as when presented to us in a striking personality. Autobiographies are also instructive reading to the student of human nature, though generally written by men who are more interesting to themselves than to their fellow men.

Q. 1. The problem raised in the passage reflects:
  (a) The material of public library
  (b) Technical process of public library
  (c) Users' need of public library

Q. 2. Public library is a centre of:
  (a) Research studies
  (b) General reading on every branch of knowledge
  (c) Specific readings

Q. 3. The clause "eminent men have always loved their Plutarch" implies:
  (a) Self-praise
  (b) Past and present
  (c) Striking personality

Q. 4. Instructive reading can be studied through:
  (a) Encyclopedias
  (b) Biographies
  (c) Autobiographies

Q. 5. The branch of study which teaches us to live the present in relation to the past is:
  (a) Biography
  (b) History
  (c) Autoiography

**Passage-7**

**Read the following passage and answer the questions:**

Emerson, over a hundred years ago, warned his countrymen in America not to imitate or depend too much culturally on Europe.... We, in India do not have to go abroad in search of the past and the distant. We have them here in abundance. If we go to foreign countries it is in search of the present, that search is necessary, for isolation from it means backwardness and decay. The world of Emerson's time has changed and old barriers are breaking down, life becomes more international. We have to play our part in this coming internationalism, and for this purpose, to travel, meet others, learn from them and understand them. But a real internationalism is not something in the air without roots or anchorage. It has to grow out of national cultures, can only flourish today on a basis of freedom and equality and trade internationalism. Nevertheless Emerson's warning holds today as it did in the past, and our search can only be fruitful in the conditions mentioned by him.... There are countries notably in the British dominions which try to humiliate our countrymen. They are not for us....

We are citizens of no mean country and we are proud of the land of our birth, of our people, our culture and traditions. That pride should not be for a romanticized past which we want to cling on to, nor should it encourage exclusiveness or a want of appreciation of other ways than ours. It must never allow us to forget our many weaknesses and failings or blunt our longing to be rid of them. We have a long way to go and much leeway to make up before we can take our proper station with others in the van of human civilization and progress.

*–Pandit Jawaharlal Nehru*

Q. 1. Problem discussed in this passage reflects mostly on:
(a) Culture of America
(b) Internationalisation of life
(c) Internationalisation of freedom and equality

Q. 2. According to the passage, real internationalism has to grow out of:
(a) Modern ideas
(b) Knowledge
(c) National culture

Q. 3. The sentence 'citizens of no mean country' means:
(a) Citizens of a backward country
(b) Citizens of low grade country
(c) Citizens of well-cultured and traditional country

Q. 4. The author wants us to:
(a) Romanticize on past
(b) Glorify our past and doing to it

(c) Initiate the west

(d) Remember a weakness and failing to find the way for a bright future.

Q. 5. The guiding force behind American self-respect and self-reliance was kindled by:

(a) Jawaharlal Nehru (b) Whitman

(c) Emerson (d) Robert Frost

**Passage-8**

**Read the following passage and answer the questions:**

Educated women have to play the role of teachers. An educated lady can serve the country in the humble capacity of a teacher. The education of children mainly depends upon women. Women can build up the character of children. Women can instruct as well as please; they can teach as well as amuse. "Human soul without education is like marble in a quarry". Women can do research work and they are winning laurels in art, literature, philosophy, music and painting. We are fortunate in having very intelligent girls who are anxious to have training in foreign countries. They are being given scholarship by the Government of India and many of them have proceeded to the U.S.A., the U.K. and Western countries and have made their mark as educationists. Women in modern India do not want to lag behind in any activity.

Women can also render social service whenever there is flood, famine, earthquake or some natural calamity. They can render social service. It is also during war that they can be of utmost utility to the nation. Knitting, sewing, embroidery, dressing, etc. can be done by the ladies. In free India, ladies are being given training in First-Aid, use of rifles and guns, and some ladies are getting training as drivers and pilots. The defence of the country is a matter of great importance to all and women should share the burden with men. In case of war, women might be asked to offer their services in theatres of war.

Q. 1. Educated women play a role of:

(a) Supervisor (b) Instructor

(c) Teacher (d) Guide

Q. 2. Women can build up:
- (a) The health of the children
- (b) The nature of the children
- (c) The attitude of the children
- (d) The character of the children

Q. 3. The sentence "Human soul without education is like marble in a quarry" implies:
- (a) Illiteracy
- (b) Without any use
- (c) No intelligence

Q. 4. In case of calamities, earthquake, flood and fire, women can render their:
- (a) Service at home
- (b) Moral encouragement
- (c) Social service
- (d) Service behind the screen

Q. 5. Women should:
- (a) Play a second fiddle to men
- (b) Rub shoulders with men
- (c) Lead the country and society
- (d) Should keep confined to domestic duties

**Passage-9**

**Read the following passage and answer the questions:**

The view is widely held that the world would be taking a long step towards goodwill among nations if it were to adopt a universal language and the advocates of this view can certainly marshal many arguments in its favour. How pleasant for the tourist, on arrival in a foreign land, to be greeted by familiar phrases. How simple for English business to word a cable that would be intelligible to an Italian, Turkish and Chinese firm; above all what harmony would come to our world if statesmen could discuss directly and accurately the problems that divide nation from nation.

We must not, however, approve an attractive idea without first exploring the difficulties involved in it. The initial difficulty in adopting a common language would be to decide what the language should be. It is unlikely that all the nations would agree on the adoption of one of the existing languages and probably the very attempt to reach agreement would sow discord among them and this defeats the ultimate purpose. The nations might prefer to create a new language, but such a language would certainly seem foreign to the first generation that employed it. When, if ever, the nations decided what language should be universal they would have to consider how it should be made so. Should children acquire it in infancy from their mothers? If so, they would probably never experience the full enjoyment to be gained from their national literature. Would it be better that the universal language should be introduced in schools as a second language in the way that many of us are now taught French or German? If so, it would continue to seem a foreign language for everyone and for ever.

If all these difficulties were surmounted and the universal language were, in fact, universally employed both in speech and writing we might expect that some misunderstandings would indeed disappear, but should we dare to think that harmony among nations was assured? People of one tongue are not always of one mind.

Q. 1. The sentence "How pleasant for the tourists, on arrival in a foreign land to be greeted by familiar phrases" applies to:

(a) National language

(b) People's language

(c) Language of majority of countries

(d) Universal language

Q. 2. Harmony of language can be achieved by:

(a) Discussion by political leaders

(b) Discussion by society

(c) Discussion by statesmen

(d) Discussion by beaurocrats

Q. 3. "The initial difficulty in adopting a common language would be to decide what the language should be:

(a) A new language common to all
(b) A language of one of the existing languages
(c) A language which is easy
(d) A language which has easy script

Q. 4. According to the passage: "When, if ever, the nations decided what language should be universal", how it should be made so?

(a) Children should acquire it in infancy period
(b) People should gain it from their national literature
(c) By introducing as second language in schools
(d) Through any of these

Q. 5. "Peoples of one tongue are not always of one mind" implies:

(a) Universally employed both in speech and writing
(b) Create misunderstanding
(c) Harmony is not assured among nations

## Passage-10

**Read the following passage and answer the questions:**

Education deprives a young person of one of the most precious possessions, the sense of co-operation with his fellows. He is like a pacifist in 1917, alone in spirit of a depressing situation, and specially, almost unbearably depressing to youth. "After all" says Duma's hero, "man is man's brother" and youth specially needs a free play of the fraternal sense; it needs the stimulus and support of association in common endeavour. The survivor of an old generation in America has had these benefits in some degree; he is more or less established and matured and can rule along fairly comfortably on his spiritual accumulation; and besides, as age comes on, emotions weaken and sensitiveness is dulled. In his day from the spiritual and social point of view, one could afford to be educated barely and with difficulty afford it perhaps but education was not a flat liability. It netted enough to be worth its price. At present one can afford only to be trained. The young persons are turning all their energies into a single, narrow channel of interest; they have set the whole current of their being in one direction. Education is all against a young person doing that, while training is all for it; home hence training puts him in step with his fellows, while education tends to leave him a solitary figure spiritually disqualified.

For these reasons, education in the first place discloses other channels of interest and makes them look inviting. In the second place, it gives rise to the view that the interest which absorbs his fellows is not worth mortgaging one's whole self, body mind and spirit, to carry on. In the third place it shows that what sort of people one's fellows inevitably become, through their exclusive absorption in this one interest, and makes it hard to reconcile oneself to the thought of becoming like them. Training on the other hand raises no such disturbance; it lets one go on one's chosen way with no uncertainty no less of confidence as a man of the crowd. Education is divisive, separatist; training induces the exhilarating sense that one is doing with others what others do, and thinking the thoughts that others think.

Q. 1. "Man is man's brother", means:

(a) Brother of evils
(b) Brother for activities
(c) Stimulus and support in common endeavour

Q. 2. "The survivor of old generation in America.... Is more or less established and matured and can rule along fairly comfortably on his spiritual accumulations" implies:

(a) Sound health
(b) Quiet atmosphere
(c) Free play of the fraternal sense
(d) Stimulus and support of association in common endeavour

Q. 3. The sentence "The young persons are turning all their energies into a single, narrow channel of interest" implies:

(a) Narrow mindedness
(b) Self-interest

(c) Single direction

(d) Narrow thinking

Q. 4. "Education is divine; separatist" as it:

(a) Discloses other channels of interest

(b) Chosen way to uncertainty

(c) Does raise disturbances

Q. 5. Professional training aims at making a man:

(a) Educated

(b) Self-centered

(c) Social but far away from real eduation

(d) Separatist

**Passage-11**

**Read the following passage and answer the questions:**

Philosophy, like all other studies, aims primarily at knowledge. The knowledge it aims at is the kind of knowledge which gives unity and system to the body of the sciences, and the kind which results from a critical examination of the grounds of our convictions, prejudices, and beliefs. But it cannot be maintained that philosophy has had any very great measure of success in its attempts to provide definite answers to its questions. If you ask a mathematician, a mineralogist, historian, or any other man of learning, what definite body of truths has been ascertained by his science, his answer will last as long as you are willing to listen. But if you put the same question to a philosopher, he will, if he is candid, have to confess that his study has not achieved positive results such as have been achieved by other sciences. It is true that this is partly accounted for by the fact that, as soon as definite knowledge concerning any subject becomes possible, this subject ceases to be called philosophy, and becomes a separate science. The whole study of the heavens, which now belongs to astronomy, was once included in philosophy; Newton's great work was called 'the mathematical principles of natural philosophy'. Similarly, the study of the human mind, which was, until very lately, a part of philosophy, has now been separated from philosophy and has become the science of psychology. Thus, to a great extent, the uncertainty of philosophy is more apparent than real : those questions which are already capable of definite answers are placed in the sciences, while those only to which, at present, no definite answer can be given, remain to form the residue which is called philosophy.

*–Lord Russel*

Q. 1. According to the passage "Philosophy...aims primarily at knowledge which gives:

(a) Unity to the body of the science

(b) System to the body of the science

(c) Unity and system to the body of science

(d) Concept of science

Q. 2. The whole passage narrates the origin and development of philosophy which:

(a) Is a kind of knowledge

(b) Is not a definite answer of the questions

(c) Gives positive results

Q. 3. According to the passage "as soon as definite knowledge concerning any subject becomes possible", this subject ceases to be called:

(a) Science (b) Psychology

(c) Mathematics (d) Philosophy

Q. 4. The whole study of the heavens (Astronomy) was once included in:

(a) Science

(b) Natural Science

(c) Mathematical principles of natural philosophy

(d) Philosophy

Q. 5. The sentence "Thus, to a great extent, the uncertainty of philosophy is more apparent than real" implies:

(a) No definite answers to its questions

(b) No truthful results

(c) No measurement of the facts

**Passage-12**

**Read the following passage and answer the questions:**

The universal tendency of human mind is to shrink from the trouble of thinking out any of its so-called opinions. People become mentally indolent, too indolent to judge for themselves. Upon every conceivable subject they take their opinions readymade. The memory thus becomes a storehouse of conventional readymade opinions and these eventually harden into irrational convictions.

People are influenced in their opinion by the prevailing fashion. They fear singularity more than error; they accept numbers as the index of truth, and they follow the crowd. The dislike of labour, the fear of unpopularity, the danger even of setting up individual opinions against established convictions, strengthen this inclination. People take their opinions from their favourite newspaper, from the accepted beliefs of the society in which they move, or of the party or church to which they attach themselves, from tradition, from custom, from hereditary association, from any source except that of careful independent thought. If they are asked why they believe a particular thing, they will say, I have it on good authority, or I read it in a book, or it is a matter of common knowledge, or everybody in the village believes it, or I learned it at school.

These replies mean that they have accepted information from others, without making any attempt to verify it, and without thinking the matter out for themselves. The causes of such beliefs are thus obvious, though such causes are clearly not reasons. But the causes may become reasons if we are able to recognize that our teachers, our family, and our neighbours are competent and truthful persons, and possess adequate information. Reasons of this kind are probably the principal ground on which, in mature life, we accept the great mass of our scientific, historical and other convictions.

Q. 1. The passage "people become mentally indolent", implies:

(a) To talk
(b) Unwilling to think
(c) To judge

Q. 2. The passage deals with dilemma of opinion of a:
(a) Individual man (b) People of a society
(c) Crowd (d) Association

Q. 3. People take their opinion from:
(a) Newspapers (b) Society
(c) Party and church (d) All above (a) to (c)

Q. 4. "People are influenced in their opinion by the prevailing fashion" whether:
(a) Wrong (b) Right
(c) There is dislike of labour (d) All above (a) to (c)

Q. 5. Causes cannot clearly be reasons if:
(a) Information is accepted from others
(b) Attempt is not made to verify
(c) Information is not valid

### Passage-13

**Read the following passage and answer the questions:**

Self-reliance is the pilgrim's staff, the worker's best tool. It is the master key that unlocks all the difficulties of life. "Help yourself and Heaven will help you" is a maxim which receives daily confirmation. He who begins with crutches will generally end with crutches. Help from within always strengthens, but help from without invariably enfeebles the recipient. It is not in the sheltered garden but in the rugged Alpine cliff where the storms beat most violently, that the toughest plants are reared. It is not by the use of corks, bladders and life-buoys that you can best learn to swim, but by plunging courageously into the waves and buffeting them.

To wait until some charitable man passes by—to stand with arms folded, sighing for a helping hand—is not the part of any manly mind. The habit of depending upon others should be vigorously resisted, since it tends to weaken the intellectual faculties and paralyse the judgment. The struggle against adverse circumstances has, on the contrary, a bracing and strengthening effect, like that of the pure mountain air on an enfeebled frame.

This is the lesson which, now-a-days, is not taught in the schools. To us it seems the vice of modern systems of education that lay down too many "royal roads to knowledge". Those impediments which formerly compelled the student to think and labour for himself are now most carefully removed, and he glides so smoothly along the well-beaten highway that he pauses not to heed the flowers on either side. The race of thorough and complete scholars is dying out. Our young men are equipped to such an extent with manuals that explain everything, and guides that go everywhere that they find no occasion for thought. Why spend an hour in grappling with an obscure passage when it is cleared up beautifully in an obliged 'note'? In a word, why take any trouble at all when so many are willing to relieve you of it?

Q.1 The phrase "Help yourself and heaven will help you", implies:

(a) Self-help (b) Selfishness

c) Self-reliance

Q. 2. The sentence "it is not by the use of corks, bladders, and life-buoys that you can best learn to swim, but by plunging courageously into the waves and buffeting them", implies:

(a) Perfect concentration

(b) Capacity to struggle with problems

(c) Self-confidence to handle the situation

Q. 3. "It tends to weaken the intellectual faculties and paralyse the judgment", if one is:

(a) Follower of others

(b) Advised by others

(c) Dependent on others

(d) Instructed by others

Q. 4. Modern education system leads to:

(a) Royal roads to knowledge

(b) Knowledge which compels to think

(c) Multiways outlook

Q. 5. Our young men are equipped with:
(a) Structural format
(b) Guiding principles
(c) No occasion of thoughts
(d) Obscure matter

**Passage-14**

**Read the following passage and answer the questions:**

There are some books, when we close them—one or two in the course of our life—difficult as it may be to analyse or ascertain the cause, our mind seems to have made a great leap. A thousand obscure things receive light; a multitude of indefinite things are determined. Our intellect grasps and grapples with all subjects with a capacity, a flexibility, and a vigour, unknown to us before. It masters questions hitherto perplexing, which are not even touched or referred to in the volume just closed. What is the magic? Is it the spirit of the supreme author, by a magnetic influence blending with our sympathizing intelligence, that directs and inspires it? By that mysterious sensibility we extend to questions which he has not treated, the same intellectual force which he has exercised over those which he has expounded. His genius for a time remains in us. Thus, the same with human beings as with books. All of us encounter, at least once in our life, some individual who utters words that make us think forever. There are men whose phrases are oracles who condense in a sentence the secrets of life; who blurt out an aphorism that forms a character or illustrates an existence. A great thing is a great book; but greater than all is the talk of a great man.

And what is a great man? A gentleman in the Windsor uniform? A field-marshal covered with stars? Is it a prelate or a prince? A king, even an emperor? It may be all these; yet these, as we must all daily feel are not necessarily great men. A great man is one who affects the mind of his generation. Whether he be a monk in his cloister agitating Christendom, or a monarch crossing the Granicus and giving a new character to the Pagan world.

Q. 1. There are some books...one or two in our course of life which are:

(a) Difficult to explain

(b) Entertaining

(c) Recommended by others

Q. 2. The sentence "It masters questions hitherto perplexing, which are not even touched or referred to in the volumes just closed, what is the magic" refers to:

(a) Printer

(b) Publisher

(c) Supreme author

(d) Supreme book

Q. 3. The phrase "Thus the same with human beings as with books" implies:

(a) Intellectual force

(b) Words that make us think for ever

(c) Reading habit

(d) Knowledge of events

Q. 4. The sentence "A great thing is a great book, but greater than all is the talk of a great man", implies:

(a) The title of the book

(b) The great man who wrote the book

(c) The man who reads the book

(d) The person who is influenced by the book

Q. 5. According to the passage, who is 'the great man'?

(a) A gentleman in the Windsor uniform

(b) A field marshal

(c) Who impacts the mind of his generation

(d) A king, even an Emperor

**Passage-15**

**Read the following passage and answer the questions:**

One of the peculiarities which distinguish the present age is the multiplication of books. Every day brings new advertisements of literary undertakings, and we are flattered with repeated promises of growing wise on easier terms than our progenitors.

How much either happiness or knowledge is advanced by this multitude of authors, is not very easy to decide.

He that teaches us anything which we know not before, is undoubtedly to be reverenced as a master.

He that conveys knowledge by more pleasing ways, may very properly be loved as a benefactor; and he that supplies life with innocent amusement, will be certainly caressed as a pleasing companion.

But few of those who fill the world with books, have any pretensions to the hope either of pleasing or instructing. They have often no other task than to lay two books before them, out of which they compile a third, without any new materials of their own, and with very little application of judgment to those which former authors have supplied.

That all compilations are useless, I do not assert. Particles of science are often very widely scattered. Writers of extensive comprehension have incidental remarks upon topics very remote from the principal subject, which are often more valuable than formal treatises, and which yet are not known because they are not promised in the title. He that collects those under proper heads is very laudably employed; for though he exerts no great abilities in the work, he facilitates the progress of others, and, by making that easy of attainment which is already written, may give some mind more vigorous or more adventurous than his own, leisure for new thoughts and original designs.

But the collections poured lately from the press have seldom been made at any great expense of time or enquiry, and therefore only serve to distract choice without supplying any real want.

Q. 1. How much either happiness or knowledge is advanced is decided by:

(a) Multiplication of books

(b) Literary undertaking

(c) Promise of growing wise

(d) Multitude of authors

Q. 2. The para 5 of the passage point out bad authorship:

(a) Books expressing new ideas and feelings

(b) Books reviewing the judgment of the former authors

(c) Books compiled out of two books taken in hand without new thoughts and material

Q. 3. The phrase "All compilations are useless" implies:

(a) Very remote from the principal subjects

(b) No authenticity

(c) No ability in the work

Q. 4. The sentence "He that collects those under proper heads is very laudably employed" implies:

(a) Experts no great abilities in work

(b) Others' progress is facilitated

(c) Considers more vigorous or more adventurous than his own.

Q. 5. The collection published lately has:

(a) Proved purposeless

(b) Served to distract choice

(c) Fulfilled real want.

Section-II

# Definitional Questions

# A

**Abstract Bulletin:** A printed or mimeographed bulletin containing abstract of currently published periodicals, articles, pamphlets, etc. issued by a special library and distributed regularly to its clientele (ALA Gloss).

**Abstracting:** It is a summary of the essential contents of a work usually and articles in a periodical together with the specifications of its locus, that is the place of occurrence, (Ranganathan). An abstract is a brief statement of the essential content of the original or indication of the characteristics of the original. It is of many kinds—inductive abstracting/descriptive abstracting; informative abstracting; annotation, slant-in abstracting; anto-abstract, graphic abstract, and telegraphic abstracts.

**Access control list:** An access control list (ACL) is a table that tells a computer operating system which access rights each user has to a particular system object, such as a file directory or individual file. Each object has a security attribute that identifies its access control list. The list has an entry for each system user with access privileges. The most common privileges include the ability to read a file (or all the files in a directory0, to write to the file or files, and to execute the file (if it is an executable file, or programme).

**Access:** Access is simply being able to get to what you need. Data access is being able to get to (usually having permission to use) particular data on a computer. Web access means having a connection to the World Wide Web through an access provider or an online service provider such as America Online.

**Accession Register:** All books procured by the library, are entered in a register called Accession Register. Accession Register may be separate for books received by purchase, by exchange and as gift.

**Accoustic Material:** Materials pertaining to sound system; phono-records, phono tapes or radio tapes are some of the (non-book) acoustic materials procured and preserved in the libraries.

**Acting Edition:** An edition of a play that gives the text as used in stage production, often in a particular production with entrances and exits and other stage business (ALA Gloss).

**ACTA:** ACTA (America's Carriers Telecommunications Association) is a lobbying organization for over 165 small long-distance telephone carrier companies. It was organized in 1985 to represent the interests of the group before legislative and regulatory bodies. The organization is based in Casselberry, Florida.

**Action Script:** Action Script is an object-oriented programming (OOP) language that is designed specifically for website animation. Action Script makes it possible for developers to create on-screen environments (such as games, tutorials, and e-commerce applications) that can respond to user input through the keyboard or mouse. Action Script is an event-based language; just as is the case in real life, actions are triggered by events.

**Adapter:** An adapter is a physical device that allows one hardware or electronic interface to be adapted (accommodated without loss of function) to another hardware or electronic interface. In a computer, an adapter is often built into a card that can be inserted into a slot on the computer's motherboard. The card adapts information that is exchanged between the computer's microprocessor and the devices that the card supports.

**Alcove System:** A method of shelving books in wall and floor cases around alcoves; the arrangement sometimes extends to more than one floor.

**Alphabetisation:** It means entries by the alphabetic order either letter by letter or word by word, in any script, viz. Roman, Devnagri, Persian, etc. Canon of consistency should be followed throughout filling of entry cards. Indian Standards Institute (ISI) has framed necessary rules for all these methods. Dr. S.R. Ranganathan has suggested 'Gestalt Alphabetisation, modified system based on Gestalt value.

**Algorithm:** The term algorithm (pronounced al-go-rith-um) is a procedure or formula for solving a problem. The word derives from the name of the mathematician, Mohammad ibn-Musa Al-Khowarizmi, who was part of the royal court in Baghdad and who lived from about 780 to 850 AD. Al-Khowarizmi's work is the likely source for the word algebra as well.

**Algol:** A computer language standardized by an international committee (Algorithmic language). It was mainly used to programme numerical publications. It is now extinct.

**Almanac:** 1. An annual publication containing calendar, frequently accompanied by astronomical data and other information. 2. An annual compilation of statistics and other information sometimes in a particular field (ALA Gloss.)

**All Over Style:** The style of book decoration which covers the whole of the side of binding, as distinct from a corner, centre or border design, whether made up of a single motif, different motifs or a repeated motif (Lib. Gloss).

**Alpha:** Alpha is both a microprocessor and the name of a computer system from the Digital Equipment Corporation (DEC), which is now part of Compaq. The Alpha processor uses a newer and more advanced architecture than DEC's flagship computer line, the VAX. The Alpha is based on reduced instruction set computer (reduced instruction set computing) architecture and handles 64 bits at a time.

**Alphanumeric:** In computers designed for English language users, alphanumeric (sometimes seen as alphameric) characters are those comprised by the combined set of the 26 alphabetic characters, A to Z, and the 10 Arabic numerals, 0 to 9. In some usages, the alphanumeric character set may include both upper and lower case letters, punctuation marks, and symbols (such as @, &, and * etc.

**Alta Vista:** Alta Vista is a popular search engine on the Web. Alta Vista can also search graphic images and tell you who is linked to your own Web pages. Alta Vista's search robot, known as Scooter, can look at and collect data from three million Web pages per day. Its indexer, Ni2, indexes one gigabyte of data per hour.

**Alternative Title:** A sub-title introduced by, 'or', its equivalent, e.g. *Twelfth Night*; or, *What You Will.*

**Amaya:** Amaya is the Web browser that was developed by members of the World Wide Web Consortium (W3C) as a practical tool as well as a testing ground for W3C ideas. Amaya includes an HTML editor as well as a viewer and can be downloaded freely from the W3C.

An API can be contrasted with a graphical user interface or a command interface (both of which are direct user interfaces) as interfaces to an operating system or a programme).

**Analog computing:** Analog computing is a term used by Paul Saffo of the Institute for the Future in Palo Alto, California, to describe silicon-based microsensors that sense and react to external (natural) stimuli in something that approximates the rhythm of reality rather than the "artificial" binary behaviour of digital computing.

**Analog:** Analog technology refers to electronic transmission accomplished by adding signals of varying frequency or amplitude to carrier waves of a given frequency of alternating electromagnetic current. Broadcast and phone transmission have conventionally used analog technology.

**Analytical Index:** (1) An alphabetical index under specific topics to information in articles arranged under general subject as in a reference book. (2) A classified index to material under specific subjects, as in a reference book (ALA Gloss).

**Analytical Notes:** The statement in an analytical entry referring to the publication that contains the article or work entered, i.e. that part of an analytical entry which is enclosed by parentheses.

**Analytical Subject Entry**: An analytical entry for an individual part of a book, entered in the catalogue under the subject with which the individual part deals. In a dictionary catalogue or alphabetical subject catalogue the entry is assigned a subject heading.

**Analytico Synthetic Classification**: A scheme which gives the classifier the maximum autonomy in construction numbers for new specific subjects not enumerated in the schedules. Ranganathan's Colon Classification is the first scheme of this kind (Lib. Gloss).

**Anonymous Classic**: A work of unknown or doubtful authorship commonly designed by little, which may have appeared in the course of time in many editions, versions and/or transactions for cataloguing purpose. The term 'anonymous classic' includes single epics, poems, romances, chronicles, etc., composite anonymous texts known under a specific title, (series of poems of romances, sacred literature, collections of legends, plays, etc.

**API**: An application programme interface (API—and sometimes spelled application programming interface) is the specific method prescribed by a computer operating system or by an application programme by which a programmer writing an application programme can make requests of the operating system or another application.

**Apocryphal Book**: (1) A book of doubtful authorship or authenticity. (2) Specifically, one of the books of the Old Testament or the New Testament Apocrypha (ALA Gloss).

**Appendix**: Additional matter included at the end of a book, supplementary to the main text and often of statistical nature.

**Apple Script**: Apple Script is a programming language that allows Macintosh users to automate repetitive tasks and to customize applications to suit specific needs. Included in every Macintosh computer. Apple Script is an integral component of the operating system that allows technically sophisticated users (not necessarily programmers) to enhance the functionality of their computers.

**Apple Share:** The Apple Share protocol is a communications protocol from Apple Computer that allows client applications in a computer to exchange files with and request services from server programmes in a computer network. Apple Share can be used over the Internet on top of the TCP/IP protocol, or on top of other network protocols such as Internet Work Packet Exchange and Apple Talk.

**Application Programme Interface:** An application programme interface (API—and sometimes spelled application programming interface) is the specific method prescribed by a computer operating system or by an application programme by which a programmer writing an application programme can make requests of the operating system or another application.

**Apupa Pattern:** An arrangement of homogenous set of compound subjects in a sequence helpful to the majority of readers and thus satisfying the laws of library science may be said to result in a Apupa Pattern—That is Alien-Penumbral, Umbral-Penumbral-Alien subjects.

**ARPANET:** ARPANET was the network that became the basis for the Internet. It was funded mainly by U.S. military sources and consisted of a number of individual computers connected by leased lines and using a packet-switching scheme.

**Artificial Intelligence:** AI (pronounced AYE-EYE) or artificial intelligence is the simulation of human intelligence processes by machines, especially computer systems. These processes include learning (the acquisition of information and rules for using the information), reasoning (using the rules to reach approximate or definite conclusions), and self-correction. Particular applications of AI include expert systems, speech recognition, and machine vision.

**ASCII:** ASCII (American Standard Code for Information Interchange) is the most common format for text files in computers and on the Internet. In an ASCII file, each alphabetic, numeric, or special character is represented with a 7-bit binary number (a string of seven 0s or 1s). All 128 possible characters are defined.

**Asiatic Society (Calcutta):** It was established in 1874 for the study and development of oriental culture and science. The building was constructed in 1804. The total collection is 150,000 manuscripts and published books.

**Assembly Language:** A low level language for programming a computer in which mnemonics are used to code operations and alphanumerical symbols is used for address.

**Atlas:** A volume of maps, plates, engravings, table, etc. with or without descriptive letterpress. It may be an independent publication or it may have been issued to accompany one or more volumes of text (ALA Gloss).

**ATM:** (Asynchronous Transfer Mode) A method of transferring messages between computers in a LAN or a WAN. It breaks up the message into fixed size packets each 53 bytes long (called cells) and finds a fixed path from source to destination through which all cells of the message travel. It is particularly suited for transmitting multimedia data.

**Attributed Author:** The person to whom authorship of a book is ascribed, there being no conclusive evidence establishing the authorship.

For cataloguing purpose such a book entered under the name of the attributed author is qualified by a phrase; such a supposed author, the authority for the authorship supposition being given in a note.

**Audio Charging:** A form of transaction charging in which details of the loans are recorded on discs or tape. The loan serial number and details of book and reader are read into a microphone and the numbered transaction card is inserted in the book as in manual transaction charging. At the overdue state, missing cards represent books not returned and the appropriate actions of record are played back and written or typed as overdue notices.

**Author:** The person, persons or corporate body responsible for the existence of the works in broader sense. Maker of the book or the person or body immediately responsible for its existence. Thus, a person who collects and puts together the writings of several authors (compiler or editor) may be said to be the author of a collection. Corporate bodies may be considered the authors of publications issued in their name or by their authority (A.A. Code).

**Author Analytical:** An entry under author for a part of a work or of some article contained in a collection (volume or essays, serial, etc.) including a reference to the publication which contains the article or work entered. (ALA Gloss).

**Author Catalogue:** A catalogue of author entries, alphabetically arranged, usually including added entries under editors, translators, etc. and entries under titles in the case of anonymous works. References are also made in the author catalogue from variant forms of author's names, from pseudonyms, etc. and parts of names not used as headings.

**Author Bibliography:** A list of the books and articles by, or by and about, an author. It follows the usual pattern of catalogue arrangement.

**Author Entry:** An entry of a work in a catalogue under its author's name as heading, whether this be a main or an added heading. The author heading may consist of personal or a corporate name or some institute for it, e.g. initials, pseudonym, etc.

**Author's Copies:** The complimentary copies of his book given to the author by the publisher, usually six copies (Book Gloss).

**Author's Edition:** 1. An edition of the collected or complete works of an author uniformly bound and having a collective titles 2. An edition authorized by the author (ALA Gloss).

**Authorised Edition:** An edition issued with the consent of the author or the representative to whom he may have delegated his rights or privileges (ALA Gloss).

**Authorization:** Authorization is the process of giving someone permission to do or have something. In multi-user computer systems, a system administrator defines for the system which users are allowed access to the system and what privileges of use (such as access to which file directories, hours of access, amount of allocated storage space, and so forth). Assuming that someone has logged in to a computer operating system or application, the system or application may want to identify what resources the user can be given during this session.

**Auto-Abstracting**: The art of abstracting, i.e. preparing an extract consisting of complete sentences from the document which is so abstracted automatically by machines.

**Autography**: (1) The author's own handwriting. (2) Reproductions of the form or outline of anything by an impression from the thing itself. (3) A lithographics process of reproducing writing, drawing, etc. in facsimile. (4) That branch of diplomatics which is concerned with autographs (Lib. Gloss).

**Autonym**: the real name of an author, and distinguished from a pseudonym.

**Auxiliary Publication**: One reproduced by the autotypes process, which as a variety of the collotype process, in which there is resin instead of gelatine (Lib. Gloss).

**AV**: AV, an abbreviation for audio/video, is frequently used as a generic term for the audio and video components and capabilities in home entertainment system and related product descriptions and reviews.

# B

**Bachelors Degree Course (B.Lib.Sc.)**: Universities conduct undergraduate degree courses or give affiliation to colleges to run such courses. Minimum admission qualification is graduate in any faculty. Course includes: History and Development of Libraries; Library and Society, Reference Services; Book Selection and Bibliography, Cataloguing; and Classification; and Information Science and Documentation.

**Back Margin**: The left hand margin of a printed recto and the right hand margin of a printed verso. In the ordinary book, the back margin is contiguous to the binding edge. Also known as inner margin, inside margin, gutter margin (ALA Gloss).

**Background Processing**: 1. The execution of lower priority programmes when higher priority programmes or real-time entries are not using system resources, the execution of lower priority programmes when higher priority programmes real-time entries are not using system resources. 2. In a multi-access system, processing that does not use online or interactive facilities in a multi-access system, processing that does not use online or interactive facilities.

**Backspace**: (1) To move a printing or display element backward one unit at a time to move a printing or display element backward one unit at a time. (2) To move one record backward in a file.

**Backup**: Any hardware, software, or data that can be retrieved in the event of system failure or user error.

**Bar Code**: A set of parallel lines of varied thicknesses and space on products sold in supermarkets. The lines represent alphanumerical characters which can be recognized and interpreted by an optical scanner. The code represented by bars is known as Universal Product Code.

**Bar-code scanner**: An optical character reader that can read data represented by bar codes and translate the codes into digital signals.

**Basic Subject**: Basic subjects are second step of main subject in the following group of mutually exclusive and totally exhaustive subjects—canonical subjects, special systems. Basic subject is a generic name used to denote either a main subject or any subject of the above three groups.

**Basic**: Beginners all purpose symbolic instruction code. A high-level interaction programming language frequently used with personal computers and in time-sharing environments.

**Bibliographer**: (1) A person familiar with methods of describing the physical characteristics of books, who prepares bibliographies, catalogues and lists. (2) One who writes about books, especially in regard to their authorship, date, typography, editions, etc. (3) One skilled in bibliography (ALA Gloss).

**Bibliographical Note**: (1) A note, often a footnote, containing a reference to one or more works used as sources for the work. (2) A note in a catalogue or a bibliography, relating to the bibliographical history or description of a book. (3) A note in a catalogue mentioning a bibliography (often in the form of footnote) contained in the book (ALA Gloss).

**Bibliography**: A list of books by one or more authors which includes brief biographical data about them.

**Bin**: A shelf divided into sections analogous to pigeonholes for the filing of periodicals. The idea is modified in periodical display stands to consist of a hinged sloping shelf under which back-numbers are filed.

**Binary chain**: A series of separate binary circuits existing in one of two possible states and so arranged that each circuit can affect the conditions of adjacent circuits.

**Binary Numbering System**: A number system with a base or ratio of 2.

**Binary word:** A fixed-length group of bits that occupies one storage location in a computer memory and is treated and transferred as a unit.

**Binary:** Pertaining to pair, as in Binary Notation System, in which only the digits, 0 and 1 are used.

**Blocking Factor:** The number of logical records, of a given size contained in a physical record, such as Block.

**Book Bin:** 1. A space in a loan desk in which books are placed while waiting for later discharging routine or pending return to the shelves. 2. Any similar receptacle in which books are kept, e.g. when withdrawn from the shelves.

**Book Card:** A card which bears details of a book and is used in recording loans. It usually carries the accession number, class number, author and title, the item used for filing appearing first in bolder type. It is put in book pocket in each book.

**Book Carriage:** A single platform, or two reciprocating spring platforms, on which a book is held by clamps for microfilming. The platform slides back and forth, on a runway to bring opposite pages of the book into the field of exposure (ALA Gloss).

**Book Entry:** A word used by L.A. Burgess to embrace in a book the precise subject matter or topic; subordinate or coordinate topics introduced; implied relationship of the books' topic with others outside the immediate scope of the book; the special locality and/or period limiting the scope of the book; the author's special point of view; the special class of readers to whom the book is addressed and the form in which it is presented.

**Book Lift:** A machine for carrying books from one floor or stack level to another, operated by hand or by power for loads of upto about 1cwt. The hand operated booklift is a simple and cheap device and may be used for vertical travel up to three tiers. Above that an electrically operated lift is used in majority of libraries of multistoreyed buildings.

**Book Mobile Service:** A service for providing library facilities to outlying stations particularly to rural community through mobile van which houses miniature library and is comparable to a part time branch library.

**Book Number:** A combination of letters and figures used to arrange books in the same classification number in alphabetical order. It usually consists of an author number, a work mark and volume of copy number. Cutter's table of author numbers and Book number formula of S.R. Ranganathan are also applied for Book numbers.

**Book Pocket:** It is pasted on the bottom of the inner right side of the front of back card board cover. It is of size 5″ × 3″.

**Book Preservation:** The functions of providing adequate facilities for the case, repair, restoration, protection and maintenance of books.

**Book Rest:** A portable wooden device similar to the music rest of a piano which is placed on a table or desk to hold a book at an angle convenient to be read.

**Book Tray:** A shallow frame for carrying a number of books, having one side and tw ) ends and provided with handles or slots in the sides for ease of handling.

**Book Trolley:** A set of shelves on wheels provided with two or three shelves, used for transporting books within the library. Adaptations are available for use in hospital libraries.

**Books of Inspiration:** Books relating to religion, philosophy, poetry, fine drama and fine fiction.

**Books of Recreation:** Books relating to fiction, drama, humour, essays and light reading in various fields.

**Bookworm:** (1) An insect which damages books by noring holes through the paper and by feeding on paste and glue, destroys the bindings, (2) A voracious reader.

**Boolean Variable:** A variable which can assume a value true or false.

**Booting:** A technique for loading a programme into computer memory in which programme's initial instructions direct the loading of the rest of programme.

**Bottom-Up Design:** A system analysis technique characterized by initiation at the detailed level, to high levels in work general terms. Contrast with top-down design procedure.

**Brackets:** 1. Rectangular marks [ ] used in cataloguing to enclose information supplied by the cataloguer or to indicate unnumbered pages in a collation. Often called square brackets to distinguish from parentheses and angle brackets. 2. Angular marks < > used in cataloguing to enclose matter which itself appears in square brackets on the title-page are called angle brackets.

**Bradford's Law:** The law deduced by Dr. S.C. Bradford (later corrected by B.C. Vickery) who found that about a third of the articles on a subject are printed in journals devoted to that subject, a further third appear in a large number of journals devoted to related subjects in an even larger number of journals in which such articles would not normally be expected to be published.

**Broadcast Network:** The communications that we have spoken about so far are two ways or interactive each part being able to transmit and receive. Broadcast network such as those operated by the BBC and IBA, are one way, meaning that only one party, broadcaster, is able to transmit, in telecommunication technology. There are direct broadcast, cable broadcast, satellite broadcast, etc.

**Brochure:** A short printed work, consisting of only a few leaves, merely stitched together with thread or cord and not otherwise bound. Literally, a stitched work (ALA Gloss).

**Brown, James Duff (1862-1914):** Librarian of Clerkenwell from 1888 to 1905, where he gained professional fame by his introduction of 'open access' in the lending library in May 1894 and where his Quarterly guide issued from July 1894, is said to have been the first annotated library bulletin in the country and of Islangton from 1905 till his death, where, often the few metropolitan Boroughlibrary systems were conceived as a whole. He made useful contribution to almost every professional topic related to library science.

**Btisnet**: It is set up by the Department of Biotechnology, Govt. of India. It is a special network linking the information, and connecting all the DRDO laboratories.

**Buffer**: An intermediate data storage area usually used to balance the different operating speeds of computer components.

**Bus Architecture**: A computer system configuration that uses a shared or multiplexed communication path between the processor and the peripheral devices, permitting multiple devices to transmit data at the same time.

**Bus**: The channel of paths between different components with a computer which help the data in connecting from one component to another is called bus.

**Business Library**: These libraries are attained with the institutions or centres established by men to carry out some specific business. It may be a trade centre or a commercial concern. Trade literature is normally received in business libraries which includes trade catalogue, patents, etc.

**Byte multiplexer channel**: An approach to connecting peripheral devices to a processor and main memory using a shared channel that transmits one byte of data at a time and interleaves bytes of data from several devices; used with slower I/O devices

**Byte**: Synonymous with character. Such byte consists of a combination of eight binary digits (bits).

# C

**C. Summer Splending:** Editor of revision of ALA code in 1960. He adopted 'statement principles' in ICCP, Paris in October 1961.

**C:** A high level programming language whose features allow one to write efficient programmes.

**C++:** A subject-oriented version of C.

**Calculator:** (1) Any device that is used to perform arithmetic operations, usually under direct operator intervention but sometimes programmable. (2) Calculating machine, specifically a small hand-held electronic device performing arithmetic operations specifically.

**Call Number:** The symbols used to indicate the location of a book on the shelve. The class number often precedes an author number which individualises the book.

**Canon of Cataloguing:** Dr. S.R. Ranganathan formulated CCC on the basis of some canons. He enunciated eight canons and a master of canons (1969). These are: (1) canon of ascertainability; (2) canon of prepotency; (3) canon of individualization; (4) canon of sought heading (5) canon of contests; (6) canon of permanence; (7) canon of currency; (8) canon of consistency; (9) canon of recall value.

**Canon of Recall Value:** It is ninth additional canon enunciated by S.R. Ranganathan in CCC in 1969. This canon is based on psychological assumptions for rendering of headings in catalogue. It is general tendency to merge the major part of the things and ideas with the passage of time and only the particular portion or part of information of maximum potency is left to remember or recall. The canon is called master canon.

**Canon:** In cataloguing, canons are termd as normative principles. Ranganathan enunciated canon in classified cataloguing code and discussed in his book *Headings and Canons* published in 1953.

**Cap Line:** Letters are formed on three imaginary framework lines, the base line, cap line and mean line. The cap line is the uppermost.

**Card Cabinet:** A case of drawers or trays in which cards are filed vertically. The front of each drawer or tray is usually fitted with the slotted frame for the insertion of a label indicating the contents. Certain card cabinets are so constructed that the drawers or trays slope downwards towards the back of the cabinet, ensuring easier consultation of the cards.

**Card Index:** An index made on cards usually of standard size (5″ × 3″) and kept on their edges in the drawers.

**Card:** A rectangular piece of cardboard, usually of standard size 5″ × 3″ (12.5 × 7.5 cm) having a surface suitable for writing, typing, etc. used in making library record intended for vertical filing.

**Carrel:** A small room or alcove for individual study in a library or in the stack, formed by partitions or arrangement of shelving in which the reader may be permitted to retain the books, notes, etc. on which he is working and where he may type or dictate his memoranda. Also called cubicle or stall.

**Cassettee (Audio):** It has standard diamension (10.2 × 6.4 cm) and features. The tape is 3.8 mm (0.15 inch) wide and in the cassette the magnetic coated surface is on the outward or exposed surface. All recorded cassettes and players run at a standard speed (4.75 cm/s). Commonly these are c 30 (15 minutes each side), c 60 (30 minutes each side), c 90 (45 minutes each side) or c 120 (60 minutes each side).

**Cassette memory:** Auxiliary magnetic tape storage media, often used to load programmes into main memory and to capture local data.

**Cataloguing Department:** (1) The administrative unit of a library in charge of preparing the catalogue, and in many libraries, of classifying the books. (2) The library quarters where the cataloguing processes are carried on (ALA Gloss).

**Cataloguing:** The process of compiling a catalogue or constructing entries for insertion into a catalogue. In a broad sense, all the processes connected with the preparation and maintaining of a catalogue, including classification, the assignment of subject headings and subject indexing.

**Catch Memory:** A small high speed memory which is used for temporarily storing a portion of a programme or data from main memory. The processor retrieves instructions or data from the main memory, instructions and data catching speeds by computation.

**Catchword Entry:** An entry for a book in a catalogue. List or index under a secondary part of its title. Used most frequently where the latter part of the title consists of significant work or phrase for which an enquirer might look.

**Catchword Title:** A partial title consisting of some striking word or phrase likely to be remembered by an enquirer.

**Caution Money:** Library receives caution money from its readers. It is charged in each and every library it lends books and other reading material. Caution money is refundable but it earns interest which is a source of income. Caution money cannot be accounted as income of the library at it is refundable.

**CAV:** (Constant Angular Velocity) Reading method used in magnetia disks. The angular velocity is same for all tracks. Thus, trucks with smaller radius have a high velocity.

**CD-ROM:** A storage technology using a laser beam to write information on an optical disk, which may then be read by a lower-power laser beam; used for archival storage of a very large volume of information. (An acronym for compact disk read-only memory).

**Central Processing Unit (CPU):** The components of a computer system with circuitry to control the interpretation and execution. It includes primary storage, arithmetic logic unit (ALU) and control unit.

**Central Processing Unit**: The part of a computer that controls the interpretation and execution of machine language instructions. It consists of a control unit, an arithmetic and logic unit, and a main memory. It is also called, central processor.

**Central Registration**: The practice of maintaining one borrower's register in a library system and including in it all readers, regardless of the service point at which they apply for library membership.

**Central Shelf List**: (1) A shelf list recording the bookstock of the main library in a library system. Sometimes called main card. (2) A combined shelf list for all books in a library system, house in the main library. Also called union shelf list.

**Chain Printer**: The printer in which the characters to be printed are embossed on a chain or a band. The chain is fashioned as a look and print heads are activated to print specified characters.

**Channel**: In data communications, a path for electrical transmission between two or more points.

**Charging System**: The method employed in a library to record the loan of books. There are many issue systems such as daybook, ledger sheets, book pockets, card system, network system, Brown system, mechanic charging machine system, computer-based system, both offline and online systems, etc.

**Chattopadhyay Committee**: Dr. Chattopadhyay Committee submitted its report to Government of India on 'National Policy on library and information system (India) in May 1986 and stressed the urgent need of networking in public libraries.

**Chip**: A thin small piece of semi conductor material on which integrated circuits have been formed, packing and connecting pins.

**Chronological Order**: An arrangement of dates (time) usually employed in subsections of a classification scheme where the material lends itself to this order, e.g. history. Works may also be arranged in chronological order of publication so that the most recent works are brought together.

**Circuit Switching:** A method of network communication in which a circuit is established between the communicating nodes for the duration of the communication.

**Circulation Statistics:** It is necessary to review the development of library services every year, Circulation statistics included the number of borrowers, readers in reference section and other sections. Necessary records are maintained in each department and development charts and tables are prepared for comparison.

**Citation Index:** These cite primary research articles on a subject by author and title. Under each citation are grouped all those contributions which have referred to the primary article. Each of an author's cited works along with the citing author and their papers, is arranged in a chronological order.

**Class Entry:** The entry of a work in a catalogue under the name of the subject class to which it belongs, as distinct from entry under its precise subject (specific entry). For example, the entry of a work on Violets under the heading Flowers or Botany rather than under Violets.

**Client/Server:** A client/server (Cs) database splits the database processing between two systems. The client PC which runs the database application and the database server which runs actual DBMS.

**Clipping:** In graphics display, the process by which the hardware or software eliminates the part of the drawing that fall outside the boundaries on the screen or a window. Also called scissoring.

**CLV:** (Constant Linear Velocity)—Recording method used in CD-ROM in which the angular velocity of the disk is deduced as the CD recording head moves to the inner tracks. This maintains constant recording density on all the tracks on the disk.

**Cobol:** Common business-oriented language. A high level language developed for business data processing applications.

**Coding:** Writing a list of instructions that cause a computer to perform specified operations.

**Collation:** That part of catalogue entry which describes the physical constitution of the work catalogued. The collation consists of three parts: (AACR) (1) Number of volumes, or in the case of a work in one volume, the number of pages. (2) The kinds of illustration including their numbers. (3) The size, i.e. height of the book when standing upright, measured to the nearest half-centimeter.

**Collection Number:** A symbol denoting any special characteristic (size, physical form, class of users, etc.) of group of books, which because of this characteristic must be separately located.

**Collective Entries:** In selective cataloguing, several entries on one card for pamphlets on the same or related subjects, they may be either all author or all subject entries.

**Collective Title:** An inclusive title for publication containing several works, is the collected work of an author or a composer, a collection of an authors or a composer's works of a certain type; or an inclusive title for the several works issued in a series (ALA Gloss).

**Collective Title:** A selective cataloguing, several entries on one card for pamphlets on the same or related subjects, they may be either all author or all subject entries.

**COM:** (Computer Output Microfilm) Normal printed output of a computer deduced to one of the several available microforms by a special output device that takes the place of line printer.

**Common Isolate:** Each division in a facet is said to be on isolate (colon classification). The isolates are of two types—special isolate and common isolate. Form divisions used by Dewey in DC are similar to common isolates. Common isolates are two types (1) Anteriorising common isolates (ACI); (2) Posteriorising common isolates (PCI).

**Common:** A facet which can offer in any of several classes of many main classes.

**Communication Channel:** A medium through which signals are transmitted and received.

**Communication channel:** The portion of a storage medium that is accessible to a given reading or writing station.

**Communication Technology:** Telecommunication means communication at distance like radio, electric currents, laser pulses. It splits into two major divisions e.g. Radio, T.V. and Telephone network. The use of carrier waves is one multiplexing, technique. Another suitable use with digital communication, splits the signals into short packets, interleaving packets from one signal with those from others.

**Communications control unit:** A small computer used to monitor and control the flow of data communications to and from the communications control unit's larger host computer.

**Compiler:** One who produces a single work by collecting and arranging written or printed material from various sources.

**Complex Classes:** A focus is complex if it comprises two or more basic classes.

**Composite Author:** A designation applied to each of the several authors contributing parts of a composite work. Distinguished from a joint author by the fact that each composite author's contribution is a separate entity, readily distinguished.

**Composite Work:** An original work produced by the collaboration of two or more authors in which the contribution of each forms a separate and distinct part, although included within the planned whole (ALA Gloss).

**Compound Name:** A name formed from two or more proper names, often connected by a hyphen, preposition or conjunction.

**Compound Subject Heading:** A subject name used as heading in a catalogue and consisting of more than one word, viz.: (1) a noun preceded by an adjective or an adjective noun; (2) Two nouns connected by a preposition or conjunction.

**Computer:** Any of a variety of electronic devices that are capable of accepting data and instructions, executing the instructions to process the data, and presenting the results. A computer typically has a central processing unit (CPU), internal and external memory storage, and various input/ output devices such as a keyboard, display screen, and printer. A computer system consists of hardware (the physical components of the system) and software (the programmes used by the computer to carry out its operations).

**Computer Mode**: One of the ordinary control modes of an analog computer that produces the time-variant solution based on the input; other ordinary control modes are reset and held. In addition, an analog computer may operate in repetitive and iterative operation control modes.

**Computer Assisted Instruction (CAI)**: Computer assisted instruction on which computers are used as tools of instruction rather than objects of instruction. CAI is defined as the use of computer to provide course constant instruction. This is known in USA as CBI—computer based instruction or computer based education.

**Computer Network**: (1) A network connecting geographically or locally distributed computers. (2) A resource-sharing network linking computers, file servers, and peripheral devices.

**Computer Operation**: (1) An electronic response by a computer's circuitry that occurs as a result of the interpretation of one of the computer's basic operation codes. (2) A basic operation built into the electronic circuitry of a computer, such as add or complement.

**Configuration**: A particular group of interconnected functional units that form a complete system or subsystem.

**Configuration**: The relationship of the hardware components of a computer system with each other, together with the electronic interconnectivities.

**Consistency**: The use in logical division of characteristics in a fixed sequence, the arrangement of coordinate classes in a fixed sequence (Ranganathan).

**Computer Network**: A group of geographical distributed computers which are interconnected using communication lines in such a way that any computer in the group may be used from any other computer location.

**Computer Security:** (Computersec) concepts, techniques, technical and administrative measures used to protect at the hardware, software and date of an information processing system from deliberate or inadvertent, unauthorized acquisition, damage, destruction, disclosure, modification or use or loss.

**Control Bus:** A set of wires used to transmit signals to control the operation of various units of a computer.

**Control Circuit:** (1) A circuit in a computer's hardware that causes the computer to execute instructions in the proper sequence. (2) A circuit used to transmit supervisory information to coordinate with transmission occurring another circuit.

**Control Key:** A key on a computer keyboard that has no meaning by itself but, when pressed simultaneously with another key, gives that key a new meaning; examples are the shift, control, and alternate (option) keys.

**Control Signal:** Any of a set of pulses used by a microprocessor to control the transfer of data over a bus; signals include read, write, request and interrupt acknowledge, bus request and bus granted, and clock input and output.

**Cooperative Acquisition:** It is an activity which has been developed and strengthened by the compilation and development of union catalogues and lists and which is undertaken by a number of cooperating libraries to provide maximum possible reading material within their limited financial resources.

**Corporate Authorship:** A work is said to be of corporate authorship when the responsibility for its contents, expression and opinions rests with a society, institution, government or some other corporate body and not with a personal author.

**CPU Time:** (1) The computational time required to execute programme instructions in a central processing unit. (2) The total amount of CPU time used by a programme.

**CPU:** Central processing unit, the part of a computer that controls the interpretation and execution of machine language instructions.

**Cross Reference:** A direction in a catalogue, from one of several headings under which an entry might be sought, to the heading adopted or to draw the attention to other headings under which related material is entered, e.g.

(1) Ornithology SEE Birds.

(2) Legends SEE ALSO Mythology, Fables, Folklore.

**Cross Translation:** A programme to translate a high level language to the machine language of some machine X and run to another machine Y.

**Cumulated Volume:** The volume of an index, catalogue or bibliography in which, at the end of a period of time, is assembled a combined sequence of entries which have appeared in earlier issues during that period.

**Cumulative Index:** An index in periodical form that at stated intervals combines new items and items in one or more earlier issues to form a new unified list, or an index to any periodical that combines new entries with those of an easier index (ALAL).

**Cutter Author Marks:** A rather elaborate method to ensure the arrangement of books, etc. in alphabetical order. To the first two and sometimes, as in the case of letter S, three letters on the author's name are added numbers. These numbers can be added to decimally facilitate the insertion of fresh names at any point.

**Cycle Time:** The time interval between the instant at which a read write command is given to a memory and the instant when the next such instructions can be issued to the memory cycle time.

**Cyclic feeding:** In character-reading equipment, a process whereby the pages of an input document are fed into the reader at a predetermined and regular rate.

**Cyclic storage:** A type of mass storage device that rotates so that data may be read or written only at the time the read/ write head is positioned over the desired physical memory location; examples are magnetic drum or disk storage devices. Also, Circulating Storage, Regenerative Storagy.

The use of carrier waves is one of multiplexing techniques. Another suitable use with digital communications, splits the signals into short packets, interleaving packets on single with those from others.

# D

**Daisy Wheel:** A disk that contains a character set on its circumference and is rotated by the printer to position the characters for printing. Also, Print Wheel.

**Daisy-wheel Printer:** An impact printer whose print elements are placed at the ends of the spokes of a rotating wheel; when the proper character is in position, a hammer causes it to strike the print ribbon. Also, Wheel Printer.

The print head in this type of printer is a 'Daisy Wheel', a circular device resembling the flower of the daisy, with the print characters embossed on the tip of each 'petal'. When printing, the wheel rotates to being the required character uppermost, and a hammer strikes it against an ink or carbon ribbon and so produces the printing impression on paper.

**Data Area:** A contiguous area of main storage, specified by its base address and size. Data within the area is referenced by the base address of the area and the offset of the data within the area.

**Data automation:** The application of computers to gathering, storing, processing, and disseminating data and information.

**Data Bank:** The majority of machine readable databases store actual information rather than reference. There are known data bank and provide answers, facts and data in response to a query. The data bank store directory type of data pertaining to business economics, social sciences, education and science and technology. A guide to databases and data banks first published in 1975 and updated regularly. Information Directory published in U.S.A. in 1980 covers 1280 database and data banks, of these 565 are bibliographical database and 715 are data banks.

**Database Management System (DBMS):** A set of interrelated software tools designed to construct and provide access to a database held on a computer system, and to control the privacy, security and integrity of data. The tools usually embody special programming languages for describing and manipulating the data known as data description and data manupulation languages respectively. They may also include a data dictionary system—a means of recording the contents of a database and how it is used.

**Data Control:** A service performed by personnel at a computing center in conjunction with quality control and computer resources scheduling.

**Data Correlation:** Data correlation is an important stage of compilation. Data gathered and grouped may have to be correlated to meet specific requirements. The correlation has to be done by linking the critical variables.

**Data Display:** The online visual representation of data, usually on a CRT screen or other video terminals under control of a computer.

**Data Integrity:** The degree of characters, timeliness, and relevance of data stored in a database indicates data integrity. Data integrity can be ensured by certain checks and validation procedures carried out whenever an update operation is attempted and also by elimination of data redundancy. Some database management systems have features which support data validation, For example, ORACLE.

**Data Sheet:** A form for collecting or recording source data that is designed for ease and convenience of transcription to machine-readable format.

**Data Slip:** Data slip is pasted on the topmost portion of the front or back fly leaf of each book. This slip is not pasted on the books kept in library for reference purpose. It is in size 5″ × 3″.

**Data Station:** The equipment at the sending location that supplies the data signals to be transmitted over a data communication channel.

**Data Structure:** A Data Structure is defined as the structural relationship present within the data. A data structure must maintain the sequence of data element and those relationships among data elements that are needed for the purpose of the System using the data. Data structures are of two types—Liner structure and Liner lists.

**Data-exchange System:** A data communication system consisting of hardware devices and data-transmission software that accepts data from one or more sources, sorts and prioritizes the data, and transmits it to one or more destinations.

**Data-handling System:** A group of automatic or semi-automatic devices that collect, transmit, receive, and store data in digital form; often used with instrumented data collection deuces.

**DDC in Online Retrieval System:** It was studied to compare an online catalogue with subject headings and found that the methods of searching were relatively equal in precision, or relevance of items retrieved; the number of relevant items retrieved, and search tir e. However, each method retrieved some different bibliographic citations in search in the same database.

**Decalcomania:** Transfer or design printed on special paper to permanent base, e.g. pottery.

**Decentralized Data Processing:** The collection and maintenance of data at individual subdivisions of an organization or at various geographical locations, each of which may be connected to any or all of the other units.

**Decimal Fraction Notation:** DC uses the decimal fraction notation. Every class number is read as pure decimal fraction. A decimal point is taken for granted at the beginning of very class number.

**Deckle Edge:** The feather rough edges of hand-made paper caused by the wet pulp flowing around the edges of the frame (deckle) which is used to press the pulp on to the mould. A similar effect is often induced in machine-made paper by special rubber deckle straps at the edge of the wire mesh or by water jets. The appearance of a deckle edge in a book is esteemed by collectors as showing the book is in its original state uncut by the binder.

**Decoder:** (1) A matrix of logic switches that selects one of the 2" character Outputs based on *n* input values. Also, Logic Deader.

**Dedication:** A statement in a book, by the author, acknowledging indebtedness or paying respect to another person. The dedication is normally brief and precedes the preface.

**Delete:** In proof correction, deletions are marked by striking out the fault in the text and by writing the correct word in the margin.

**Delhi Public Library:** It is a well-equipped library of India established in 1951 in Delhi as a Public Library pilot project by Ministry of Education, Govt. of India in collaboration with UNESCO. It concerts Central Library, 28 branches and a Braille department for the blind, children section and a mobile library network and deposit stations. The library has a collection of 7 lakh volumes in 5 languages, namely Hindi, English, Urdu, Punjabi and Bengali. It has one lakh members.

**DELNET:** DELNET is one of the experiments that are now ongoing in the country to network libraries in big metropolitan cities. DELNET will network thirty-five libraries in Delhi area. Participating libraries create databases of their monographs and serials holdings using CDS/ISIS. All databases created co-operatively are expected to reside on a central computer system and dial up access provided to all participating libraries.

**Demco Self-charging System:** A simplified version of the Network charging system which dispenses with entries on the readers' tickets. The borrower enters his own ticket number on the next line of the book card and the assistant checks this entry and stamps the date label.

**Demy:** A standard size of paper 17½ × 22½". (printing). Drawing and writing paper, 15½ × 20". Also called small demy.

**Denotation (Classification):** The aggregate of objects of which a word may be predicated, (O.E.D.) as distinguished from connotation.

**Dentelle:** Lace-like tooling on the borders of a book cover, placed near the edges and pointing towards the centre.

**Denudation:** The formation of sub-class by the addition of a differentiate to the parent class.

**Department Work:** A term used by cataloguers to indicate a work by one author which is related to some previous publication by another author, the latter work being either a modification or augmentation of the earlier, e.g. abridgements, adaptations, commentaries, concordances, continuations, dramatizations, indexes, librettos paraphrases, parodies, revisions, selections, sequels, and supplements.

**Departmental Catalogue:** A catalogue containing entries for books in one department only of a library.

**Departmental Issue Method:** The periodicals pertaining to a particular subject or department are transferred to a concerned department which keeps the periodicals for long period generally up to the time when the volume is completed and then it is bound and kept in library.

**Depository Library:** A library which is entitled by law to receive free copy of every book published in the country and wherefrom document or information of specified description may be supplied.

**Depth Classification:** The carrying out of classification, so minutely, in such depth that the most specific subject in all its aspects is identified.

**Descender:** (1) That part of a lower case letter which descends below the body of the letter. (2) Used of the whole letter which has a descender.

**Descriptive Bibliography:** Descriptive bibliography is also the application of analytical bibliography to the physical form of a book. It aims to describe an ideal copy of a particular edition, describing all variations from this ideal norm.

**Descriptive Cataloguing:** That part of the cataloguing process concerned with the identification and description of a book as distinct from the determining of the subject, its subject headings or subject indexing. It provides full description of book.

**Descriptor:** It is a team or a set of terms used to surrogate the concept. It is an expression listed in the sources. A term has only one meaning within its subject field and authorized for use in co-ordinate indexing.

**DESINET:** It is developed by DESIDOC for the DRDO units, and covers the Defence Scientific and Research Information and comments all the DRDO laboratories, scattered throughout India. Desinet is a proposed bibliographical information network for defence, covering only unclassified scientific and technical information. The user of DESINET would be scientific, research and defence personnel from the Deptt. of Defence, Deptt. of Defence R&D and Deptt. of Defence Production and Supplies.

The Defence bibliographical network will also have close links with other network like NICNET for exchange of information.

**Desktop Computer:** A microcomputer that is small enough to be placed conveniently on an office desk.

**Destination Slips:** Paper slips inserted into newly purchased books in the book-order or cataloguing department. Part of the slip is left projecting and by its colour and/or making indicates the library and department to which the book is allocated.

**Detroit Self-charging System:** A simplified form of the Network charging system which eliminates certain steps and requires the borrower to enter his ticket number on the book card.

**Devices:** Dr. S.R. Ranganathan was inclined to make colon classification scheme with much more hospitality in array and chains. The hospitality is ensured with the help of devices like chronological devices, geographical devices, subject devices, superimposition devices, Mnemonics device and alphabetical device.

**Dialogue**: The interaction or conversation between a computer and the users. Also, dialog.

**Dial-up line**: A telephone line connected to a modem that allows access to a computer or network via the telephone system.

**Diazo Process**: A transmission method of photocopying exploiting the property of certain dyes of the Diazo group which are sensitive to light. Also known as the dyeline process. Diazo paper being much cheaper than silver halide papers is often used for taking copies from an 'autopositive' master. In libraries the process may be used for taking copies of a master catalogue entry typed on a thin translucent paper.

**Dickman Charging System**: An American device, also adopted by some British libraries, to record book loans by machine. An ordinary book card is used but the reader's ticket has an embossed number. The ticket and card are inserted in the machine to stamp the reader's ticket number on the book card and record the loan.

**Dictionary**: Dictionary contains words of a language or subject arranged in alphabetical arrangement giving their meaning, spelling, pronunciation and derivation. The word lexicon, thesaurus, word book, vocabulary and glossary are also used as synonyms for dictionary. It is of many types—language dictionary, subject dictionary, special purpose dictionary like spelling dictionary, synonyms dictionary, dictionary of new words, etc. There are many important dictionaries like *New Websters International Dictionary*, *Oxford English Standard Dictionary* which are internationally known. *New Websters International Dictionary* is in 3 volumes.

**Die-Stamping**: Printing in raised letters by an intaglio die, either with ink or in blind stamping, without ink. The latter process is used for Braille books, and also in book-binding, for ornamentation.

**Digest**: (1) A brief condensation of a written work, often in other words other than those of the original. (2) In law, a compact summary of laws, reported cases, decisions, etc. systematically arranged (ALA Gloss).

**Digital Computer**: A machine that can be programmed to accept digital data, carry out arithmetic, transfer, and logic operations on the data, and supply the results in a useful form. In modern terminology, generally called a "computer".

**Digital Data Recorder**: A device that records information as discrete values on a recording medium; occasionally includes an analog-to-digital conversion capability.

**Digital Display**: A visual output consisting of character and numeric representations of digital data; especially as distinguished from analog display, such as a waveform on an oscilloscope or an indicator on a dial or scale. Also Digital Readout.

**Digital Integrator**: A device that calculates definite integrals in which the input and output variables are represented digitally.

**Digital Printer**: A narrow line printer used in industrial applications to create a permanent continuous record of numerical values, such as temperature or pressure, shown by an instrument over a period of time. Also, *Journal Tape Printer*.

**Diplomatic(s)**: The study of official documents, annually early documents, including handwriting and chancery practices, for purpose of authentication (ALA Gloss).

**Diptych**: An ancient, hinged writing tablet consisting of two tablets of wood, ivory or metal covered with wax on the inside surface, on which writing was done with a stylus (ALA Gloss).

**Direct Access**: (1) The ability to enter or access data directly in any location on a storage device, without reference to previously entered or accessed data. (2) Relating to or employing this capacity to locate data directly. Thus, direct-access memory, direct-access storage device, direct-access library.

**Direct Data Entry**: The input of data directly into a storage device from machine-readable source documents or by means of an online terminal, such as a key-to-disk device.

**Direct Input/Output:** The transfer of data between computer main memory and input/output devices without the use of buffers.

**Directory:** A list of persons or organizations, systematically arranged, usually in alphabetic or classified order, giving address, affiliations, etc. for individuals, and addresses, officers, functions and similar data for organization (ALA Gloss).

**Discursive Information:** Information is a message conveyed or intended to be conveyed by a systemized body of ideas. Discursive information is characterized by one or more of the following attributers relating to its treatment and/or expression, ranging over a wide field and proceeding logically or coherently from topic to topic.

**Disk Drive:** An electromechanical unit that spins a magnetic disk and controls the read/write heads for direct access to stored data.

**Disk:** A direct access medium used for high volume auxiliary memory, composed of a circular plate coated with magnetic material; the disk rotates under and is accessed by one or more read/write heads.

**Diskette:** A flexible plastic disk coated with magnetic material and used as an inexpensive storage medium for micro-computers and minicomputers. Also, Flexible Disk, Floppy Disk.

**Display Cycle:** The time required to completely refresh a visual display screen.

**Display Processor:** The part of a computer system that is dedicated to the control and display of information on a CRT screen.

**Display Work:** A term applied to the use of type in unconventional combinations and faces with a view to attracting attention as in advertising.

**Dissecting for Colour:** Matter to be printed in two or more colours is first set up as if for one colour. A proof is taken and the matter for each colour is separated into individual phases using the proof as guide for position. The black block is usually the key block on which other colours are registered.

**Dissemination:** The distribution of information either on request or not, to members of an organization by librarian or information officer.

**Dissertation:** A written treatise or the record of a discourse on a subject, prepared and presented in part fulfilment of the conditions for the award of a degree or diploma. Nowadays, a dissertation is most often a single written treatise by an individual, presented as the final requirement before the degree is awarded.

**Distribution:** (1) Breaking up the lines of type after printing and their return to the appropriate portions of the case. In machines such as Linotype, the metal is melted. (2) The speading of ink on the printing forms.

**Document Bibliography:** It is a list of embodied macro and/or micro ideas—that is, of book and/or of articles in periodicals—on a specialized subject or an any number or on even all the subjects. Document bibliography means the preparing of such a list.

**Document Handling:** The process of submitting a single-sheet document for character reading; it includes loading, feeding, transporting through the reader, and unloading.

**Document:** (1) A record containing information readable by a person or a machine. (2) To record information about a computer programme, system, or package for use during development operation or maintenance.

**Documentation Services:** It is a process of reproducing any available material and making it available to readers. It includes documentation list, reprographic services, translation services, union catalogue and reference service.

**Documentation Work:** It is the technique of collecting, cataloguing, classifying and abstracting of both published and unpublished material. It includes acquisition, selections, indexing, classifying, arranging and compilation of list.

**Documentation:** The organized and accessible set of recorded information needed to define and develop a computer-based system, to operate and maintain a package, programme or system, and to maintain a record of changes to an operational system.

**Donations:** Public and academic libraries receive donations from public for its functioning particularly for building books. Donation is also an income source of library.

**DOS:** (1) An operating system first developed by IBM for their small and intermediate-sized 360 model computers. (2) A generic term now referring to microcomputer operating systems that use magnetic disks, either hard or flexible, as primary online storage. (An acronym for disk operating system).

**Dot matrix printer:** An impact printer that forms characters as a pattern of closely spaced dots, each printed dot resulting from the actuation of a pin in the print head before impact with the print ribbon, the number of pins is a measure of the print quality. Also, dot character printer.

Dot-matrix printer and the daisy wheel printer described in the next section, are character printers, which means that these print one character at a time.

**Dotted Print:** A relief process of engraving in which the parts cut in relief print and tonal values are rendered by punching small dots through the plate. Also known as Manierch crible, Schrotblatt (Lib. Gloss).

**Double Title Page:** (1) A term used for two title-pages that face each other, as in many German books; as a rule, one is for the series or set of volumes as a whole, the other for the particular volumes in the series or set (cf. ADDED TITLE-PAGE); (2) A title-page that occupies two facing pages, also called double-spread title-page.

**Doutype:** Two half-tone plates produced from the same original both made from the same half-tone negative, but etched separately to yield different colour values when superimposed.

**Dry Point:** A process of engraving in which the line is incised on the plate by a solid piece of steel sharpened like a pencil and used similarly. No acid is used. The displaced metal is thrown to one side and retaining ink, produces a pleasant tone round the line when printed. Only about 50 prints may be taken before a degeneration. Often combined with etching.

**Dummy:** (1) A sample copy of the proposed work made up before printing with the actual materials, i.e. paper and covers and cut to the correct size to show bulk, style of binding, etc. A dummy usually contains a specimen printed page to show suggested type and is useful for estimating costs; (2) A piece of wood or some other material used to replace a book out of its regular position, on which is placed a label indicating the location of the book. Also called 'shelf dummy'. (3) In a file or a catalogue, a piece of paper or cardboard on which is indicated the location of material filed elsewhere or temporarily removed (Introd. Typogr., ALA Gloss).

**Duplicator:** A machine designed to produce multiple copies by means of a stencil or by means of the offset or hectographic processes. In the first process, the stencil, of waxed fibrous material, is 'cut' by typing without a ribbon and placed on a cylinder covered by an inkpad. Ink is pressed through the cylinder evenly and is forced through the openings in the stencil on to blank paper fed into the machine. Early duplicators were of the flat-bed type and the ink was pressed through to the paper by means of a rubber hand-roller. Stencils may also be prepared by drawing or writing on the stencil with a special stylus or by electronic methods.

**Dust Wrapper:** The loose paper wrapper or jacket covering the casing of a modern book, usually bearing the title, author's name, often an illustration and advertising matter designed to increase sales of the book.

**Dynamic Map:** One which expresses movement such as transport, migration or military manoeuvres. The symbols used are mainly flow lines and arrows (Lib. Gloss).

**Dynamic Storage:** A volatile type of semiconductor memory in which the binary digit is stored as a charge on the ground capacitance and must be refreshed at regular intervals. Also, Dynamic memory.

# E

**Edition:** All the copies of a book, magazine or newspaper, produced except for minor alternations, from one setting of the type.

**Editor Reference:** A reference in a catalogue from an editor's name, or from an entry under the editor of a work to another entry where more complete information is to be found (ALA Gloss).

**Electric Bibliography:** A list of 'best books' and useful as a guide for selecting books for the average library, whether retrospective or current, the items cited are acknowledged to be best in their fields.

**Electronic Data-processing Center:** A specified area used to contain a computer, its peripherals, and the personnel operating the data-processing system.

**Electronic Data Processing:** Computer can be considered to be an extension of punch-card equipment. It was first developed in 1950. It has input and output equipment, storage unit, Central unit to interpret the stored information and direct their execution and arithmetic and processing unit. Electronic Data Processing System (Computer) has two categories of work: (1) Key boarding, updating, deleting, sorting, printing, distributing, calculating, merging, filing; and (2) Sorting. Computer system has following auxiliaries —paper tape, magnetic tape, magnetic disc, magnetic cards, magnetic drum, printer, optical character reader, magnetic ink, character reader, closed circuit television.

**Electronic Mail:** Electronic mail is an application in which any user on a network can send/receive letters on his computer terminal to/from any person in the work who has an electronic mail address.

**Electronic Typewriter:** A typewriter whose input is provided by an operator, but whose output is produced by electronic components.

The print head on electronic typewriter is normally daisy wheel and a computer interface may be provided, enabling these machines to serve both as a daisy wheel printer and a typewriter.

**Electrotype:** A place made by the electrolytic deposition of copper on a mould of wax formed from an illustration block, e.g. a wood engraving which when mounted on wood to type height, may be used in place of the original.

**Elliot, John (1831-1911):** First Librarian of Wolverhampton from 1869-70 until his death and secretary of science classes organized by the Wolverhampton library committee. Invented the first widely known system of visible loan recording, the Elliot indicator, consisting of columns of small shelves, each shelf bearing the call number of a book, into which was inserted a thick and prominently coloured readers, ticket when a book was issued, i.e. the first combination of a public 'indicator', showing the reader which books were available, and a charging system.

**Emblem Book:** A type of book in which designs or pictures called emblems, expressing some though or moral idea were printed with accompanying proverbs, motto or explanatory writing, or in which verses were arranged in symbolic shapes such as crosses (ALA Gloss).

**Encoder:** (1) Any device capable of producing machine-readable output. (2) In character recognition, a printer designed to print forms, with certain type fonts in certain positions on the forms. (3) A logic circuit, the opposite of a decoder, that converts a signal on one of many lines into a binary code representing the line on which the signal occurred.

**Encyclopaedia:** A comprehensive work presenting the state of knowledge at a given time concerning the universe or concerning a subject or group of subjects. Most great encyclopaedia provide comprehensive information under the appropriate heading and in view of the general availability of these works, it is unnecessary to repeat this information in the present volume. Readers are particularly recommended to study the excellent entries in Brockaus and Britannica and to read the very fine general and historical survey of encyclopaedia by S.H. Steinbery.

*Encyclopaedia Americana*: (New York, American Inc.) It is a comprehensive encyclopaedia in English language. It provides index volume to facilitate the user in finding out specific information easily and quickly.

**Entry Word**: The word by which an entry is filed in the arrangement of a catalogue or bibliography, usually the first word of the heading other than an article. Also called filing word or a unit product of bibliographic description is an entry. It is always a documentary source of information.

**Ephemera**: (1) Current material, usually pamphlets and clippings of temporary interest and value; (2) Similar material of the past which has acquired literary or historical significance (ALA Goss).

**Ethernet**: A high-speed local area network using coaxial cable, broadcast transmission, and variable time delays in the event of a collision.

**Ethernet**: A standard for local area network connected (IEEE802) which uses a carrier sense multiple access with collection detection (CSMA/CDS) protocol.

Differing views on what constitutes evolutionary order have caused much difficulty among classifiers and the problem is probably insoluble.

**Evolutionary Order**: In classification, the arrangement of subjects in the order in which knowledge, and therefore, its record, may be said to have originated or evolved.

**Experimental Data**: Experiments from one of the most important procedures for the generation of data in science and technology. The experiments are usually planned and are designed to obtain data for specific goals and purposes.

**Extension Card**: A catalogue card that continues an entry from the preceding card. Often called continuation card.

**Extension Service:** Activities of library service which are undertaken for dissemination of knowledge by ways and means with the object of reaching groups of people who might otherwise be unaware of the library. Such activities include reading circle discussion groups, lecture societies and provision of books for prisons, clubs, hospitals, library societies, etc.

**Ez-Net:** Ez-net offers total CD-ROM network solutions. Ez-Net is a turnkey CD-ROM Network that is designed to be installed and operated by the average person, with little or no computer knowledge. It is shipped preconfigured and tested, so that it can be straightaway plugged in and install the CD. The acess time to any CD's library. Ez-Net has full compatibility to multimedia and meets the MPC2 standards. It is an expensive system. It includes Ez-station.

# F

**Facet Chain**: Facet analysis of Ranganathan provided derivation of consistent approach to subject heading and yet provided flexibility to assign subject heading co-extensive to the specific subject of the documents. The principles of facet sequence would determine the sequence of correct rendering of the specific subject headings and the reference headings.

**Facet Syntax**: The facet syntax derived on the basis of the postulates and principles particularly the wall-picture principle of the general theory of library classification in the same for each subject in each language, which is in the conceptual order and independent of linguistics syntax, although the linguistic syntax defers from language to language.

**Facsimile**: A faithful reproduction of a manuscripts or printed documents. A reprint of a work in the same or similar type is not usually referred to as a facsimile, the term applying properly to reproductions made by photographic or lithographic processes. A facsimile may be smaller or larger or the same size as the original.

Fascimile or fax, was developed at the turn of the century to transmit image such as newspaper photographs by telephone line. A fax machine contains a photoelectric cell which scans the image and concerts the blacks, grays and whites into electric signals and modulates the telephone carrier wave. The machine will also act as a receiver, able to decode incoming signals and print them as an image on special paper.

**False Date**: The date (usually the imprint date) given in a book wrongly by delay in publications, intentionally, or by error.

In a catalogue entry such a date will be quoted, the correct date is also being given in the following form: 1953 (i.e. 1954).

**False First Edition:** An edition called 'First edition' by a publisher when there has been a previous edition issued by another firm (ALA Gloss).

**Festschrift:** A complementary and memorial publication in the form or a collection of essays, addresses and biographical, bibliographical, scientific and other contributions, often embodying the result of research, issued in honour of a person, an institution or a society, usually on the occasion of anniversary celebrations. (ALA Gloss).

**Fictitious Imprint:** An imaginary imprint used for the purpose of evading legal and other restrictions, to mask piracies, to protect anonymity of the author, etc. Sometimes called False Imprint. The catalogue entry for the book bearing a fictitious imprint may quote this in the conventional imprint order. Where the actual imprint details are ascertained these follow the fictitious imprint, enclosed in brackets.

**File-storage Unit:** A high-capacity secondary memory component of a computer system, such as a magnetic disk or tape unit.

**Film Strips:** The film strip is a collection of images organized in different forms. They are stored in a binder with a flap of notes and cut-out hole in a pad of spouge rubber for the canisters. Variations on this formation of complete cardboard boxes. It is in single or half frame/double or full frame. Colour: Black/White.

**Filter:** A device or routine that separates signals or data in accordance with pre-specified criteria. (1) A machine word containing a specific bit pattern used to select, test, or extract parts of other machine words. (2) A programme that selects some data from a set, while removing others.

**Finding List:** A list of books of a special kind or by a particular writer, represented in a library or in the libraries within a given area. The purpose of the finding lists is to show whether a particular title is represented and to indicate where each may be found. The entries are, therefore, brief, consisting usually of author's name, short title, edition, date and location symbol. A finding list of books in various localities is more often called union Finding List.

**First Line Index**: An index to poetry, songs, hymns, etc. in which entry is made under the first line of each poem, song.

**First Vertical**: On a standard ruled catalogue card, the vertical line farthest to the lift, at which the author heading begins.

**First-Word Entry**: A catalogue entry made under the first word (other than an article) of a book's title. A title entry.

**Five Fundamental Categories**: Dr. S.R. Ranganathan divided the universe of knowledge in main classes and canonical classes and each class divided by more than one train of characteristics. Each train of characteristics gives rise to one facet of the universe. These facets in the field of knowledge were all manifestations of Five Fundamental Categories—Time, Space, Energy, Matter and Personality. These five fundamental categories are symbolized as 'P' for Personality, 'M' for Matter, 'E' for Energy, 'S' for Space and 'T' for Time in colon classification.

**Flexowriter**: A device resembling a typewriter that was used with early computers to accept paper tape input.

**Foldings**: A general term referring to the folding of a sheet of paper to form a section. The following are the usual foldings:

Folio (Fo) 4 pages.

Quarto (4to) 8 pages.

Sexto (6to) 12 pages.

Octavo (8vo) 16 pages.

Duodecimo (12mo) 24 pages.

Sextodecimo (16mo) 32 pages.

Ocrodecimo (18mo) 36 pages.

Vicesimo-quarto (24mo) 48 pages.

Trigesimo-secundo (32mo) 64 pages.

**Folio**: (1) Format: a book printed on full size sheets folded medially once, making two leaves, or four pages; (2) Also the form (proportions) resulting from such a folding; (3) A single leaf especially in a manuscript.

**Foolscap:** A standard size of printing paper measuring 13½" × 17". The name is perhaps derived from the watermark of a foolscap and bells used for this size of old papermakers.

**Footnote:** Matter supplementary to the text placed at the base of the page but within the type area. Set in type two points smaller than the text. Reference marks serve as link between the text and the note.

**Footprint:** The outline and surface area occupied by a computer and its peripheral equipment on the floor or desktop.

**Ford Foundation Grant:** It is given since 1951 for library development of university libraries. Special grant was given to Delhi University library where Dr. Carl M. White visited as consulted to study working of its university library.

**Forecasting:** Forecasting is one of the factors of library management. It is an estimate of the future condition. The forecast is based on the statistics technique and indexes and provides a base of information which develops specific operating plans. Forecasting is the calculation of reasonable probabilities about the future.

**Forename Entry:** Entry in a catalogue under the personal name of an author, as distinct from the more usual entry under surname of family name. Saints, sovereigns, ruling princes and members of the immediate families of sovereigns, popes, persons known under first name only, are entered under forename. The majority of oriental writers are also entered under the personal name.

**Form Card:** A card used in catalogue that bears a printed or mimeographed statement applicable to many books, sets, headings, etc. with space for the edition for further information (ALA Gloss).

**Form Division:** Dewey employed a series of more form divisions with minor alternations. These are used with the same meaning throughout the scheme wherever specific instructions appear and the practice may be added to other numbers, if the bulk of the literature on that subject require it.

**Form Entry**: The entry of a work in a catalogue under a heading expressing (a) the form in which its subject material is organized as a periodical or dictionary (b) its literary form as poetry, drama, etc.

**Form Heading**: A heading used for form entry in a catalogue, e.g. encyclopaedia, periodicals, poetry, short stories, sometimes called 'form subject heading'.

**Format**: A term defining the size and shape of a book. (1) The number of times the original paper has been folded to form leaves of the book, e.g. folio (folded once), Quarto (folded twice), Octavo (folded three times), etc. Less strictly, the general proportions and approximate size of a book, etc. which would result from such folding. (2) Loosely, the general appearance and physical make-up a book, etc. including proportions, size, quality and style of paper and binding, typographical design, margins, illustrations, etc.

**Formatted Tape**: (1) A magnetic tape reel that has been initialized and prepared to accept data. (2) A magnetic tape that contains a direct reference to recorded blocks of data; a desired block of data can be accessed by transporting the tape media at high speed to the proper location on the tape.

**Form-feed Printer**: A hard copy output device that prints on continuous paper.

**Forward-backward Counter**: A special-purpose register that can be either incremented (forward counting) or decremented (backward counting).

**Fugitive Material**: Material printed in limited quantities and usually of immediate interest only at the time of, or in the place of publication, such as pamphlets, programmes and nearprint material (ALA Gloss).

# G

**Galley Proofs:** Proofs pulled from type in galleys. The stage at which corrections are most easily made by the author, for lines may be altered without disturbing page allocation as would be the case with substantial changes in page proof.

**Gateway:** A functional unit that connects two computer networks based on common network protocols and that supports routine; for example, LAN gateway, and mail gateway. The computer networks may be local area networks, wide area networks, or other types of networks.

**General Information Reference:** A general direction is a cue, from specific subject on which the library has no individual books, to the general subject which includes the specific subject.

**General Reference:** In cataloguing a particular kind of 'see also' reference giving a general direction to the kind of heading under which one may expect to find entries for particular kinds of names. Often used as a blanket reference to replace several specific references. Also called general cross-reference and information entry.

**Generation:** (1) Any of the groups used to classify computers historically, according to such features as their hardware components, logical organization, or programming techniques; thus, first-generation, second-generation, etc. (2) Any of a family of files, each one a modification of the next most recent file. (3) In micrographics, a measure of the remoteness of the copy from the original copy, which is referred to as the first generation.

**Genetic Algorithm (GA):** A procedure that selects pairs of descriptions from a population of descriptions, applies genetic operations (such as crossover and mutation) to these pairs to produce offspring, evaluates the members of the resulting population by some criteria to select the surviving population, and then repeats the procedure. Genetic algorithms are used in genetic learning for example, in forms of machine learning to evolve rules of behaviour. The term 'genetic' comes from the field of natural genetics, where it is linked to heredity, variation of the species, and the survival of the fittest.

**Geometric Configuration**: In computer graphics, a set of features that describes the spatial characteristics of an image or part of an image. The spatial characteristics may include qualitative features, such as squared, circular, etc. or quantitative features such as area, perimeter, dimensions.

**Gigabit**: One billion bits.

**Gigabyte**: A unit of storage capacity equal to $2^{30}$ (roughly, one billion) bytes.

**Gigaflop**: One billion floating-point operations per second; used as a measure.

**Global Area Network (GAN)**: A network that comprises computer networks on an international scale.

**Global**: Pertaining to a language construct that is within the scope of all modules of the programme.

**Glove Input**: In virtual reality, the gestural input of the hand that is monitored through a glove fitted with sensors along the fingers and translated into computer commands that are reflected in a virtual world.

**Goper**: It lets user to prowl through the Internet by selecting resources from menus.

**Gopher**: A menu-based information searching tool that allows users to access various kinds of databases, such as FTP archives. Gopher is an early form of an Internet browser. Gopher software uses the client-server model.

**Gopherspace**: The part of the cyberspace to which the user has access by means of Gopher software.

**Government Libraries**: There are libraries managed by government funds which are known as government libraries.

They are of many types, but fall into three broad groups—national libraries and other libraries of national importance, departmental libraries; and special research libraries, mainly (but not entirely) in scientific, technical, medical and agricultural fields.

**Graph***:* A representation of any sort of relationship by means of dots, lines, curves, etc. in the field of various disciplines.

**Group Routine Method**: The periodical is circulated by the members of the group among themselves and on a fixed date it has to be returned to the library from where it is issued to another group.

**Guard Sheet**: As used on the catalogue card, a leaf of paper (usually thinner than that on which the remainder of the book is printed) bearing descriptive letterpress or an outline drawing, inserted to protect and elucidate that plate or illustration which it accompanies. The guard sheet is not normally included in the pagination. If the descriptive letterpress is printed on the same kind of paper as the remainder of the book, the term leaf may be used. (ALA Gloss).

**GUI**: A type of computer interface consisting of a visual metaphor of a real-world scene, often of a desktop. Within that scene are icons, representing actual objects that the user can access and manipulate with a pointing device. GUI is pronounced "goo'-ee" and is the abbreviation for graphical user interface.

**Guide Card**: A card, having a projecting edge or tabs at the top suitable labelled, inserted in a card file to indicate arrangement and facilitate the finding of entries. Guide cards are usually made of thicker, heavier stock than that used for the entry cards, also being distinguished by their different colour. Different lengths and positions of projecting tabs are obtainable termed wholes (or singles) centre halves, side halves, thirds, fourths and fifths.

# H

**Hacker:** (1) Originally, any person having highly technical computer skills, such as an assembly language programmer or a systems programmer. (2) A popular term for a person who experiments with computer-system hardware, software, and communications, sometimes without proper authorization.

**Half-tone Screens:** Transparent plates ruled diagonally with opaque lines at right angles to each other. The thickness of the line and the intervening space and approximately equal. Screens need not be ruled at $90^0$, nor the ruling need be plain lines. Interesting effects are obtained by broken, curved or variegated screens, but the customary screen is the $90^0$ angle and only varies according to the fineness of the result required, i.e. in the number of rulings to the inch.

**Hand-made Paper:** Very fine quality paper made in individual sheets, on a moulding tray which is dipped in furnish composed of linen rag fibres. Careful drying, sizing and maturing combine to make a very durable, stable paper suitable for high-class book production.

**Hard Drive:** A disk drive that reads and writes data on hard disks; it is internal in some systems but may also be connected to an external port. Also, hard-disk drive.

**Headline:** (1) A line at the top of the page giving the brief title or chaper heading (see also RUNNING TITLE, CAPTION). (2) A line especially on the front page of a newspaper showing the subject of the article in extra large type.

**Hierarchical Memory:** A computer architecture incorporating multiple kinds of memory, with the fastest and most expensive memory such as cache memory at the tope of the hierarchy and slower, more voluminous, and less expensive memory at lower levels.

**Home Address:** An address written on a track of a direct-access volume, such as a disk or drum, to identify the track's address relative to the beginning of the volume.

**Home Computer:** A personal computer adapted or intended for use in the home for non-professional applications.

**Horizontal Flow Chart:** A flow chart that shows the movement of tapes, forms, and other recording media through an organization, for the entire lifecycle of the media.

**Host Computer:** (1) The central computer in a distributed computer system that provides service to remove terminals or computers. (2) In micro-programming, the matching that interprets programmes written in other machine languages. (3) In multiprogramming, the machine responsible for allocating storage and I/O resources to virtual machines that are dependent upon it. Also, host processor.

**House Journal:** A periodical publication produced by an industrial or commercial organization for circulation to staff and/or customers. It carries mainly technical information rather than personal or social news which is usually published in the House magazine. Outstanding examples are the *Ciba Review*, *Far and Wide* (Guest, Keen and Nettlefold), the *De La Rue Journal*, etc.

**Hub:** A socket on a control panel or plugboard into which an electrical lead may be connected in order to distribute signals to multiple sites.

**Hybrid Computer:** A computer that has both digital and analog capability.

**Hybrid Interface:** A device that connects a digital computer to an analog computer and performs the analog-digital conversion of signals.

**Hybrid Processing System:** A distributed processing system that has both hierarchical and horizontal organization and control.

**Hybrid System**: A computer system that is capable of performing two or more unrelated functions, such as word processing and monitoring of laboratory equipment, in real time.

**Hydraulic Computer**: A computer in which valves and fluids are used in place of electronic circuitry.

# I

**Illustrator Entry**: A catalogue entry under the name of the illustrator of a book. Where a book consists solely or chiefly of illustrations this entry is the main entry, the illustrator being considered the 'author' in its widest sense. Should the illustrations be secondary in importance to the text the main entry is made under the author of the text, the illustrator entry being an added entry.

**Image Processing**: Computer operations on graphic image data; pictorial information is both input and output.

**Image**: (1) The exact duplication of data in a different medium, such as a screen display of the contents of computer memory. (2) In graphics, the output form of a graphics file.

**Image**: The deposit of silver or other chemical by which a picture is formed. The latent image is the invisible image formed by the action of light on the sensitized paper or film. This image becomes visible on developing.

**Impression**: (1) The whole number of copies of a work printed at one time from one setting of type. Several such impressions may be taken in one edition, either from type of stereo plates, a new edition only arising if substantial alterations are made in text or the imposition of pages is changed; (2) Of engravings, the print taken from the engraved plate by means of the special engraving press.

**Imprint Date**: It indicates the year of publication as specified on the title-page or publisher's statement. It does not necessarily give the actual date of publication owing to the trade custom of pre-dating, e.g. autumn books.

**Index Register**: A register in CPU whose contents are added to the operand address specified in an instruction to find an effective address in memory form where the operand will be fetched.

**Information Files**: (1) A file containing pamphlets and other material useful for miscellaneous information, arranged for ready reference. (2) A card file of reference area, expert in assessment and interpretation of the literature.

**Information Media**: There are two types of information media. Conventional medias are catalogue. Non-conventional media is documentation service, communication technology and computer technology.

**Information**: It is sometimes used to mean knowledge. Any recorded data may be called information. Man's experience, ideas, observations, experiments recorded in manuscripts, books and journals, films, tapes, discs and computer files.

**Input Register**: A special-purpose shift register that receives serially transmitted data and retains it until a complete word is accumulated, then transfers the data to a buffer, another register, or internal storage. Also, input buffer register.

**Input Station**: Computer or intelligent terminal that is linked with a central computer system to feed manufacturing data directly to a processor, enabling real-time processing of the data.

**Input/Output Buffer**: A block of storage used to transfer data received from a peripheral unit to and from main memory.

**Input/Output Control Unit**: The logic and connectivity needed to initiate and control the flow of data to and from a specific input/output device.

**Input/Output Controller**: A separate logic processor that provides a high-speed interface between peripheral devices and main storage, including buffer operations, channel selection, scheduling, and interrupt handling.

**Input/Output Device**: A unit that sends data to the computer for processing or that receives data from the computer, or both.

**Input/Output Interrupt**: An external hardware interrupt caused by an input/output device requesting a transfer of data (input) or signaling the completion of transfer of data (output).

**Input/Output Switching:** The allocation to a peripheral unit of more than one channel for communication with the central processing unit.

**Input/Output Traffic Control:** The controlled time-sharing of a computer's memory among peripheral devices and the central processor, allowing simultaneous input/output operations to occur.

**Input/Output:** (1) The transfer of data between a computer and a peripheral device. (2) Of or relating to equipment, techniques, or media used for this processing. Also, I/O.

**Interactive:** Describing a system or programme that maintains an exchange with the user, alternately accepting input and then responding. Thus, interactive graphics, interactive information system, interactive processing.

**Interface Card:** A type of circuit board that connects external devices to computers.

**Interface:** The physical or logical connection between a computer and the user, a peripheral device, or a communications link.

**Inter-Library Loan Method:** It is impossible for one library to purchase all books and non-book material published or produced in whole world and also not possible to accommodate them at one place. But it is the duty of the library to provide reading facilities and made available all books housed in other libraries also. Inter-library loan method makes it practicable through reciprocal basis. Libraries send their reading material to each other on loan for a particular time and bear the postal charges.

**Internet:** (1) Any network that connects other networks. (2) Internet, a large network of this type that covers the U.S. and extends to Canada, Europe, and Asia, providing connectivity between governments, universities, and corporate networks and hosts.

**Internet:** A world wide network of computers. Several thousands of individual computer networks are inter connected to form the internet. Internet provides electronic mail, telnet (remote logic to computer), file transfer services and enormous amount of information to various discussion groups and information retrieval facilities.

**Inverted Heading:** The heading of a catalogue entry with the natural order of words transposed e.g. (1) Chemistry, Organic (2) Agriculture, Ministry of. Inversion of headings is normally made when some word other than the first is decidedly more significant and is likely to be sought by enquirers. Inversion of compound subject headings is also frequently adopted by small libraries in order to bring related aspects of a subject together and for the fact that the subsequent grouping in the catalogue frequently differs from the classified arrangement of the books on the shelves.

**Inflibnet:** It is a network programme established by University Grants Commission (UGC) for university and college libraries in the field of computerization. About 30 university libraries are using computers for library function. Many other are in process. Most favourable areas are circulation, acquisition, cataloguing, serial control, reference service, bibliographical database and budgeting. INFLIBNET activities include computerization and automation of libraries and information centres, up-skilled library staff, creation and augmentation of database and establishment of communication network. Its headquarter is in university campus, Ahmedabad.

# J

**Java:** An object-oriented language which is easily portable. It is normally used to programme on the Internet.

**Jha Committee:** The government of India appointed a Review Committee in 1968 under the Chairmanship of Dr. V.N. Jha to review the working of the National Library, Calcutta. It recommended an acquisition and conservation of all national production of printed material, collection of oriented material, acquisition of foreign material, rendering of bibliographical and documentation services of current material.

**Job Specification:** The term job-specification is used for the personal characteristics required for the job. Whether library is small or large, it has been the responsibility of proper staffing once we know what that job is, we must determine what kind of person we need to do the job. Job specification is a major tool in the staffing process.

**John Dury:** (1595-1680) He was a Librarian of Kings Library. His two letters published under the heading 'The reformed library-keeper' stressed the librarianship to channelise the sources of knowledge to keep update enquiries. He wanted university libraries to be centre of scientific and literary interest. He suggested book acquisition policy.

**Joint Authorship:** Applied in cataloguing to those cases where a book is the joint production of two or more authors writing in collaboration, the parts written by each not being specified. Works of joint authorship are entered by the chief catalogue codes under the author whose name appears first on the title page, with references or added entries for the second and following authors, i.e. joint author.

**Journal**: 1. A chronological record of data processing operations. The journal may be used to reconstruct a previous or an updated version of a file. 2. Loosely, synonym for log. 3. In database management systems, the record of all stored data items whose values are changed as a result of processing and manipulation of the data.

# K

**Kernel:** The part of the operating system that provides its most basic functions.

**Key:** (1) In organization of data, an identifier that is part of a set of data elements. (2) In computer security, a variable-length bit string that controls the operations of encryption or decryption. (3) On a keyboard, a manually actuated mechanism that performs a specific operation or causes the display of a particular character.

**Keyboard Printer:** A simple input/output device combining a keyboard and a printer that echo-prints the keyed-in data; also used to display computer output.

**Keyboard:** A set of keys, such as on a user terminal, text processor, or typewriter.

**Key-disk Machine:** A data entry machine in which data entered via a keyboard is recorded directly on a magnetic disk.

**Key-driven Calculator:** An electromechanical desk calculator, now considered obsolete, in which the digit keys, arranged in columns, drive the accumulator dials for displaying results.

**Keypad:** A small group of keys that are set up for convenience and greater flexibility such that they are clustered together physically on a keyboard. For example, a numeric keypad or a cursor control keypad.

**Knowledge Acquisition:** The process of locating, collecting, and refining knowledge and converting it into a form that can be further processed by a knowledge-based system. Knowledge acquisition normally implies the intervention of a knowledge engineer, but it is also an important component of machine learning.

**Knowledge Management:** The systematic management of the knowledge processes of creating, identifying, encoding distributing, and applying information across on organization.

**Knowledge:** 1. An organized, integrated collection of facts and generalizations. 2. Information representing human experience and expertise. The knowledge built into an expert system includes facts, events, and rules.

**Knowledge-based System (KBS):** A computer system that provides for solving problems in a given field or application area by drawing inferences from a knowledge base. The term "knowledge-based system" is sometimes used synonymously with "expert system", though it is usually not restricted to expert knowledge. Some knowledge-based systems have self-learning capabilities.

**Kothari Commission:** The Education Commission under the chairmanship of Dr. Daulat Singh Kothari said that no educational institution should be established without taking into account its library needs in terms of books, staff, journals, and space.

**KWIC:** (Key Word Indexing Context). It is a machine device widely used to produce the indexes on computers. This method was developed by IBM; KWOC is refined form of KWIC.

# L

**LAN Gateway:** A functional unit that connects a local area network to another network using different protocols or where more control is desired than that provided by a simple router. The network may be another local area network, a public data network, or another type of network.

**LAN Multicast:** Sending of a frame that is intended to be accepted by a group of selected data stations on the same local area network.

**LAN Server:** A data station that provides specific services to other data stations on a local area network. For example, a file server, print server, mail server.

**LAN:** Local area network is an interconnection of many computers and terminals located within 10 km radius via a fast communication link.

**Language Preprocessor:** A functional unit that effects preparatory processing of programmes. For example, a macrogenerator may function as a language preprocessor of a translator.

**Language:** (1) A set of symbols, characters, utterances, gestures, conventions, and rules for conveying information (2) In computer programming, a set of characters, conventions, and rules for constructing expressions and for the interpretation of these expressions.

**Laptop Computer:** A battery-powered portable computer small enough and light enough to be operated on a person's lap.

**Laser Disk:** An optical disk, typically 12 inches (30 cm) in diameter. Contrast with compact disk.

**Laser Printer:** An electrostatic printer that uses a laser beam for image formation. Laser-beam printer, commonly called 'laser printer', is page printer, meaning that it prints an entire page at a time. It is very fast and silent in operation.

**Laser Scanner**: A functional unit that moves a spot of laser light across an object and creates an image from the reflection observed.

**Learning by Analogy**: A learning strategy that combines inductive learning and deductive learning so that inductions determine the common characteristics of concepts being compared or associated, and deductions derive the features expected of the concept being learned from these characteristics. Learning by analogy requires the ability to recognize the similarity between two problems and to use rules developed in one problem space in order to solve a problem in another problem space.

**Learning from Solution Paths**: Reinforcement learning that relies on waiting until a complete solution path for a problem has been found, marking every move along the solution path as a positive example, and marking every move leading directly off the solution path as a negative example.

**Learning Rate**: In artificial networks, a parameter that regulates the magnitude of changes to connection weights during learning. The amount of change of a connection weight is the product of a value given by the learning algorithm and a coefficient which is the learning rate.

**Learning**: (1) The process by which a biological or an automatic system gains knowledge or skills that it may use to improve its performance. (2) The process by which an artificial neural network improves its performance by adjustment of its parameters in response to succession of input patterns. In general, learning consists in connection weight adjustments.

**Ledger System**: This system is maintained for entry of periodicals received in library. Periodicals are entered in an subject-alphabetical order and each periodical is allotted one page. Index is given in the beginning of ledger. It is in prescribed proforma. Printed ledgers are available.

**Legal Deposit**: Legal deposit, copyright deposit, the copy tax or the delivery of printed copies, as it is severally termed, is a method whereby one or more privileged libraries in a nation state, province, union or empire regularly receive free copies of all newly published books from the publishers or printers in that region.

**Letter:** A graphic character that, when appearing alone or combined with others, represents one or more concepts of a written language, or one or more sound elements of a spoken language. Diacritical marks used alone and punctuation marks are not considered to be letters. Synonymous with alphabetic character.

**Library Committee Meeting Agenda:** All problems and proposals, enlisted and circulated among the library committee members before the committee meeting for discussion in the meeting is called agenda of the committee.

**Library Committee Minutes:** Decisions of library committee meeting written according to the sequence of the meeting agenda and finally signed by the members of library committee attended.

**Library Fee:** It consists of fee received thorough annual fee, causal readers fee and other membership fee. It is non-refundable fee and a source of revenue of a library.

**Library Hour:** The timings of opening and closing the library and the hours in between the two in a week day, are called library hours.

**Library:** A collection of related files, for example, a set of inventory control files in stock control.

**Limited Edition:** An edition issued with relatively small number of copies, to which consecutive numbers are generally assigned; sometimes issued with superior paper or binding, in addition to regular edition. A special page often states the facts of editing limit and the number, and contains also the signature of the author or printer (ALA Gloss).

**Line Printer:** A printer that prints a line of characters as a unit.

**Line Spacing:** The distance between the baselines of successive lines.

**Linear Network**: A network in which there is a single principal path that includes all nodes of the network such that all other paths are subpaths of this principal path. A linear network is a special case of a tree network.

**Link**: (1) A network component used to connect two nodes directly. The link may be unidirectional or bi-directional. (2) To interconnect data objects by establishing pointers or to interconnect portions of one or more programmes by providing links, for example, to link object programmes by a linkage editor. (3) A part of a programme, often a single instruction or address, that passes control and possibly parameters between separate modules of this programme.

**LISP**: An applicative programming language oriented to list processing, recursion, and character string manipulation and logic; it is widely used for artificial intelligence applications and is based on the lambda calculus of mathematical logic. LISP is the abbreviation for list processor.

**Literature Search**: Particularly in a special library, a systematic and exhaustive search for published material bearing on a specific problem or subject, with the proportion of abstracts for the use of the researches of abstracts, for the use of the researcher; as intermediate stage between reference work and research, and to be differentiated from both (ALA Gloss).

**Local Area Network (LAN)**: A computer network located on a user's premises within a limited geographical area. Communication within a local area network is not subject to external regulations. However, communication across the LAN boundary may be subject to some form of regulation.

**Local Transformation**: In computer graphics, image transformation in which the value of a pixel is modified based on the value of its neighboring pixels; for example: convolution, mathematical morphology. Synonymous with neighbourhood processing.

**Log**: (1) To chronologically record data about events. (2) To record automatically data concerning attempts by the system to query or to update a database. (3) Loosely, synonym for journal.

**Logger:** A functional unit that records events and physical conditions, usually with respect to time.

**Logic Circuit:** A circuit that performs operations following the rules of symbolic logic; for example, a circuit whose input and output signals represent quantities that may assume values from a finite set of discrete values.

**Logic Programming:** A method for structuring programmes as sets of logical rules with predefined algorithms for the processing of input data to a programme according to the rules of that programme.

**Logical record:** A record whose data elements are related from a logical viewpoint, independent of their physical environment. Portions of one logical record may be located in different physical records, or several logical records or parts of logical records may be located in one physical record.

**Logical Ring:** The simulation of a ring network by passing a token between data stations in a predefined sequence, even though the network's physical architecture may be different, such as a bus network.

**Logical Schema:** (1) A part of a database schema that pertains to the logical level. (2) the part of the internal schema that pertains to the logical level and that, therefore, is a part of the database schema.

# M

**Machine Language**: An artificial language composed only of the machine instructions of a specific computer or class of computers.

**Machine Learning**: The process by which a functional unit improves its capability or performance by acquiring new knowledge or skills, or by reorganizing existing knowledge or skills.

**Macro Library**: A collection of macrodefinitions available for use by a macrogenerator.

**Macrogenerator**: A module, often part of an assembler or compiler, that replaces each macroinstruction or macrocall in a source programme with the appropriate code in accordance with the corresponding macrodefinition.

**Macrolanguage**: (1) A programming language designed to define macrodefinitions and macroinstructions. (2) A programming language that includes macrodefinitions and macroinstructions.

**Macroprocessor**: A subprogram provided in some assemblers and compilers to support macrodefinitions.

**Magnetic Card Storage**: A magnetic storage in which data are magnetically recorded on the surface of thin flexible cards.

**Magnetic Disk Storage**: A magnetic storage in which data are magnetically recorded on the flat surfaces of one or more disks which, in use, rotate around a common spindle.

**Magnetic Disk**: A flat circular plate with a magnetizable surface layer on one or both sides of which data can be stored.

**Magnetic Drum Unit**: A device that contains a magnetic drum, the mechanism for moving it, magnetic heads, and associated controls.

**Magnetic Drum**: A right circular cylinder with a magnetizable layer on which data can be stored.

**Magnetic Storage**: A storage device that uses magnetic properties of certain materials. Magnetic techniques may also be combined with other techniques such as in magneto-optical storage.

**Magnetic Tape Storage**: A magnetic storage in which data are magnetically recorded on the surface of a tape that moves longitudinally when in use.

**Magnetic Tape**: A strip of magnetic material that is suitable for recording data for subsequent machine reading.

**Magneto-optical Disk**: A rewritable optical disk providing for data to be written as marks in the form of magnetic domains in the recording layer and erased from it using the thermomagnetic effect, and read using the magneto-optical Kerr effect. Synonymous with MO disk.

**Mail Gateway**: A functional unit that connects two or more dissimilar message handling systems and transfers messages between them.

**MAN**: Metropolitan Area Network.

**Mandatory access control (MAC)**: In computer security, a means of restricting access to objects, based on the sensitivity, as represented by a sensitivity label, of the information contained in the objects and the formal authorization or security clearance of subjects to access information of that sensitivity, and enforced by the trusted computing base. Contrast with discretionary access control.

**Margin**: Blank part of the page outside the text area. The four margins are named head or top; fore-edge, the outer or side; back, inner, inside or gutter. The proportions accepted for book work are that the bottom is double the top, and the inside margins a half or two-thirds of the outer margins. These proportions are fundamentally those revived by William Morris.

**Marginal Notes**: Annotations in the side margins of the page. Also side notes, handing shoulder notes, marginalia.

**MARC**: The Library of Congress launched a pilot project in 1966 for machine readable cataloguing data. The pilot project called MARC-I ended in 1968 and was followed by a permanent subscription service called MARC-II. By subscribing to this service, a library can acquire, in machine readable form (such as magnetic tape), cataloguing data for American as well as foreign publications. In actual practice, it means that the central organization catalogues the documents, records the data on magnetic tape and supplies libraries with copies of the tapes. MARC-II format has been adopted and developed by British National Bibliography (BNB) in cooperation with Library of Congress.

**Master Card**: A main entry in a card catalogue hearing tracings indicating all the added entries, including subject entries, and all references whether from forms of name or from subjects, used in respect of the work catalogued, together with a note of the sources used and other information pertinent to its cataloguing.

**Master Catalogue**: A catalogue, usually the official union card catalogue of a library system and situated in the central library or the cataloguing department, in which every main entry is a master card. The master catalogue, normally maintained by the cataloguer, is the official up-to-date record of catalogued stock and an essential source of information for the cataloguers.

**Master Degree in Library Science**: Universities conduct master degree course or give affiliation to colleges to run such course. Minimum qualification for admission is Bachelor's degree in Library Science (B. Lib. Sc.). The course includes advance study of cataloguing, classification, information technology, bibliography, universe of knowledge, networking, computer application in libraries and communication medias.

**Master Station**: In basic mode link control, the data station that has accepted an invitation to ensure a data transfer to one or more other stations. At a given instant, there can be only one master station on a data link.

**Mathematical Morphology:** An image algebra whose variables are shapes and whose operations transform those shapes. Synonymous with morphology.

**Matrix Storage:** Storage whose elements are arranged in such a manner that access to any location requires the use of two or more coordinates; for example, cathode ray storage.

**Matrix:** (1) A rectangular arrangement of elements, arranged in rows and columns, that may be manipulated according to the rules of matrix algebra. (2) By extension, an arrangement of any number of dimensions. (3) In computers, a logic network in the form of an arrangement of input leads and output leads with gales connected at some of their intersections.

**Mechanical Mouse:** A mouse whose movement is converted into signals by interpreting the movement of a wheel-and-bushing system.

**Medium Access Control Protocol:** In a local area network, the protocol that governs access to the transmission medium, taking into account the topological aspects of the network, to enable the exchange of data between data stations.

**Medium Interface Connector (MIC):** In a local area network, the connector used to attach a data station to a trunk coupling unit, trunk cable, or drop cable.

**Medlars:** (Medical Literature Analysis and Retrieval System of the National Library of Medicine, USA) is the highly sophisticated computer-based system designed to achieve knowledge of other bibliographies to provide current awareness services.

**Memory Card:** Deprecated synonym for flash memory card.

**Memory:** (1) Any of the addressable storage space in a processing unit or any other internal storage that is used to execute instructions. (2) All of the addressable space in internal storage. (3) Loosely, synonymous with the main storage, however, in calculators, microcomputers, and some minicomputers, the term "memory" is preferred to the term "main storage".

**Message Handling**: A distributed information processing task that integrates the intrinsically related subtasks of message transfer and message storage.

**Message Identification Service**: A service that enables the message transfer system to provide a user agent with a unique identification for each message or probe submitted to or delivered by the system, for example, a time stamp.

**Message Storage**: In electronic mail, the automatic storage of messages for later usage within the message handling system.

**Message Switching**: A method whereby messages to be transmitted between computers are all sent to a central computer, which gathers them and routes them to the appropriate destination(s).

**Message Switching**: In a data network, the process of routine message by receiving, starting as necessary, and forwarding complete messages. Contrast with circuit switching, packet switching.

**Message Transfer Agent (MTA)**: A functional unit of the message transfer system that conveys messages to users or to groups of users identified by distribution lists.

**Message Transfer System (MTS)**: A functional unit consisting of one or more message transfer agents that provides store-and-forward message transfer between user agents, message stores, and access units.

**Message**: (1) A quantity of data that is complete in some sense and that has been transferred, or has been structured for such transfer, from one entity to another for interpretation and action. (2) In information theory and communication theory, a sequence of characters intended to convey information. (3) In programming languages, a request for an object to perform one of its operations. (4) In electronic mail, an information object transferred between user agents. A message usually consists of two parts—content and header.

**Metacompiler**: Synonym for compiler generator.

**Metadata:** Data about data, including their data descriptions, ownership, access paths, access rights, and data volatility.

**Meta-knowledge:** Knowledge about the use and control of domain knowledge.

**Metalanguage:** A language used to specify some or all aspects of another language and possibly itself; for example, Backus-Naur form.

**Microcard:** A registered trade name for 5" × 3" micro opaque card bearing a bibliographical heading in normal size print. The latest microcard is now issued double sided with the catalogue heading on one side only.

**Microcomputer:** A digital computer whose processing unit consists of one or more microprocessors, and includes storage and input/output facilities.

**Micro-Document:** Micro-document means documents other than books and likewise physical form. Micro document includes articles of periodicals publications, chapters or parts of books, etc.

**Microfiche:** A sheet of macrofilm capable of containing micro-images in a grid pattern, usually containing a title that can be read without magnification.

**Microfilm:** (1) A high-resolution film for recording microimages. (2) To record microimages on film.

**Microfilm:** Microfilm probably the best known as it is used extensively by industry for the preservation of records. There are at present three standard widths of film, 16mm (0.6"), 35mm (1.3") and 70mm (2.8"). For library work the roll is normally in 100 ft length and it is the least expensive form of producing a single copy edition. The manuscript is microfilmed and the negative stored.

**Microform:** A medium, such as microfiche or microfilm that is suitable for recording microimages.

**Micrographics:** Technology concerned with methods and techniques for converting any form of information to or from microform.

**Microprint**: A micro-opaque card produced by the offset printing process, and manufactured under the trade name of Reader Microprint. The 6″ × 9″ cards are kept in cloth-bound slip cases and each card bears an eye legible heading. An extensive publication programmer has been initiated covering a wide range of subjects. Newspaper, periodicals and out of print books have all been included.

**Microprocessor**: A processor implemented as single integrated circuit.

**Micropin**: A tiny pin embedded in a glove output device or a body suit that transmits, sensations of pressure, texture, or tangibility to a wearer coming in contact with virtual objects.

**Modem**: A functional unit that modulates and demodulates signals. Frequently, a modem is used to enable digital signals to be transmitted over analog transmission facilities. The word "modem" is a contraction of Modulator-DEModulator.

**Module**: (1) A part of a programme developed to be discrete or identifiable with respect to actions such as compilation, binding, or execution, and that may interact with other programmes or parts of programmes. The concept referred to by the term "module" may vary according to the different programming languages. Synonymous with programme unit. (2) In an information resource dictionary system, a set of capabilities that may be required or optional.

**Motion Study**: It is a process that determines the work standards. The motion study is a science eliminating the wastefulness, ill-directing and inefficient motions. In making the motion study, the librarian should select the task of study.

**Mouse Pad**: A surface on which a mouse can be moved, typically a rectangular pad covered with fabric to improve traction.

**Mouse Pen**: A pen-like pointing device that is operated by dragging its tip on a surface or by directly tapping it on a screen.

**Mouse Tray**: A small and flat tray designed to contain the movements of a mouse by its operator and often having a wrist-rest.

**Mouse:** A hand-held pointing device operated by moving it on a surface other than the display surface. A mouse is usually equipped with one or more push-buttons for selecting items, or instigating action on the screen. Contrast with trackball.

**Mouse:** It is small plastic box maintained on two metal wheels whose axes are at right angles. The mouse is moved around on a flat surface called a tablet. As the mouse is moved, a cursor on the screen is moved and (x, y) coordinates of the cursor may be determined.

**MS DOS:** Microsoft disk operating systems designed by Microsoft Corporation for IBM compatible personal computers.

**MS-Windows:** An operating system with good graphical interface and multitasking facility developed by Microsoft Corporation for PCs.

**Multicomputer:** A computer including two or more main processes that communicate with each other, each having its own add space.

**Multidimensional Language:** A language whose expressions assembled in more than one dimension, such as flowchart logic diagrams, block diagrams, and decision tables.

**Multifocal Subject:** A document may deal with multifocal subject which may be broken down into component compound subjects going with the basic subject. A separate entry is to be prepared for each component subject.

**Multimedia:** (1) Pertaining to the combined use of more than type of media. A multimedia presentation may combine auto text, two and three dimensional graphics, still pictures, moving pictures. (2) The domain of multimedia concept applications, and techniques, applications, and techniques.

**Multiple Access:** Any technique whereby a number of data stated are able to share a resource in a predetermined manner, in accordance with traffic demand. Examples of shared resources are: a bus in a local area network, a satellite transponder.

**Multiplex:** To interleave or to transmit concurrently two or more signals on a single transmission channel.

**Multiplexer**: In data communications, a functional unit for assembling signals from separate sources into a single composite signals. Synonymous with data multiplexer.

**Multiplexing**: (1) A process for combining signals from several separate sources into a signal for transmission over a single transmission channel. (2) In OSI, a function within a given layer by which more than one connection of this layer is supported by one connection of the next lower layer. The term "multiplexing" is also used in a more restricted sense to refer to the function performed by the sending entity while the term "demultiplexing" is used to refer to the function performed by the receiving entity.

**Multiprocessing**: All-operating mode that provides for simultaneous processing of tasks by two or more processors of a multiprocessor.

# N

**Name Authority File:** A file, usually on cards, listing the forms of name of both personal and corporate authors, editors, etc. authorized for use as headings in a catalogue, together with an indication of the reference to be made from variant forms or other parts of each name.

**Name Catalogue:** An alphabetical catalogue of entries under the names of persons and places as author headings and as subject headings. The name catalogue in the same manner as an author and title catalogue, with the addition added entries under the names of persons and corporate bodies when these are treated as the subject of books.

**Name Reference:** A reference from an alternative form of a name to the form selected for use as a heading in the catalogue.

**National Information System:** A system which achieves national objectives though economic and effective utilization of information in technological innovation, decision-making, research and education.

**National Union Catalogue:** A cumulative author list representing Library of Congress printed cards and titles reported by other American Libraries. Publication of this was started in 1948.

**Natural Language:** This refers to a human language as opposed to a computer language. While computer languages such as C++ or Java are very structured and designed to be clear in meaning to a parser, natural languages evolved over thousands of years and took on characteristics like accents, slang, inflection, local terminology and meaning of words and phrases in context. The understanding and use of natural languages is a much harder problem for computers than understanding computer languages.

**Network Adapter Card:** An expansion board that enables a computer to connect to a network over an electrical cable, or a fibre optic cable, by radio, or with infrared light.

**Network Agent:** In network management, a functional unit that is capable of performing management operations on managed objects and of emitting notifications on behalf of managed objects. Synonymous with network assistant.

**Network Analyzer:** A functional unit that monitors the activity on a network to support performance analysis or troubleshooting.

**Network Browser:** A programme for the navigation over a computer network. This programme formats and displays information from the network in a form suitable to the user. A network browser may work in a text-only mode or in a graphical mode. Synonymous with net browser.

**Network Management Server:** A server that provides network administrative or network management services.

**Network Management:** The monitoring and controlling of components of a computer network, including the configuration of the network, and the allocation of resources across the network.

**Network Operating System (NOS):** An operating system that makes a collection of independent computers act as one computer system. Features may include centralized login and reallocation of resources across the network.

**Network:** An arrangement entities and their interconnections. In network topology or in an abstract arrangement, the interconnected entities are points on a scheme, and the interconnections are lines on the scheme. In a computer network, the interconnected entities are computers or data communication equipment, and the interconnections are data links.

**Networking:** The processes involved in managing, operating, or using computer networks.

**Node:** (1) In a network, an entity that is associated with or connected to one or more other entities. In network topology or in an abstract arrangement, the nodes are points on a scheme. In a computer network, the nodes are computers or data communication equipment. A network may contain end nodes and intermediate nodes. (2) In a data structure, a point from which subordinate items originate. A node may have no subordinate items and is then called a terminal node. (3) In a data network, a point where one or more functional units interconnect transmission channels or data circuits.

**Noise Burst Signal**: In a token-bus network or a token-ring network, a signal indicating that there is activity on the transmission medium that does not result in a valid frame.

**Noise**: A disturbance that affects a signal and that may distort the information earned by the signal.

**Nonimpact Printer**: A printer in which printing is accomplished by some means other than mechanically striking the printing medium. Examples of non-impact printers are inkject printers, thermal printers, and electrostatic printers.

**Nonprocedural Language**: A programming language that provides the means to state what is to be achieved by the actions of a data processing system without giving specific statements or instructions to be executed in a specific sequence.

**Notation**: It is a symbol which stands for the classes and their sub-divisions: a shorthand sign or symbol standing for the name of a term, forming a convenient means of reference to the arrangement of the classification scheme. Notation is necessary to hold together the table of classification scheme, and should convey a representation not merely of the division, but also of the sequence, logic or artificial, so far as it can be expressed. Dr. Ranganathan has divided notations in two kinds—pure notation and mixed notation.

**Null Modem**: A cable that enables two computers to communicate without the use of modems.

**Numerical Control** (NC): A technique of operating machine tools or industrial processes, the motion or sequence of which is determined by numerically coded commands. These commands may be generated by a computer-aided design and manufacture system on a data medium that controls a machine tool or an industrial process.

**Numerical Database:** A numerical database is defined as non-redundant, multi-usable independent and physically available set of data elements. A data element is a specific unit of information.

# O

**Object-oriented Language**: A programming language that supports object-oriented concepts, for example, Eiffel, Smalltalk, C++, Java.

**Object-oriented Programming (OOP)**: The term usually refers to programming languages that allow you to work with objects. These objects can contain not only data type and data structure information, but also information about how the object can be used by procedure.

**Online Analytical Processing (OLAP)**: Analytical processing by using a multidimensional view of data to analyze performance by product, region, market, over time and to move up and down the hierarchies of each dimension.

**Online Service**: A commercial service that (for a price) provides goodies such as e-mail, discussion forums, tech support, software libraries, news, weather reports, stock prices, plane reservations, even electronic shopping malls. To access one you need a modem. Popular online services include America Online, CompuServe, and prodigy.

**Online Transaction Processing (OLTP)**: This refers to a group of programmes that allow real time inputing, recording and retrieval of data to/form a networked system. The speed of recording the data is critical, as is the reaction time of the system so that people entering data are not bogged down.

**Online**: (1) Pertaining to the operation of a functional unit when connected to and able to interact with another functional unit. The other functional unit is usually senior in some respect. An example is a personal computer connected to a computer network. (2) Pertaining to user access to a computer via user terminal.

**OPAC:** Stands for Online Public Access Catalogue. An automated catalogue system. The catalogue is stored in machine-readable form, and accessed online by the library clientele via a VDU and employing user-frinedly software.

**Open Access:** In open access, books are kept on open shelves and reader can handle them freely and directly. Many a reader is unable to enunciate his requirements in exact terms. Open access will increase the chance for every reader to get his book.

**Open Database Connectivity (ODBC):** This is a standard API for communicating with database servers. There are different ODBC drivers supporting most of the major database servers, such as Oracle and Microsoft SQL Server. If you programme to ODBC, you get the advantage of being able to easily use your application on different databases without reprogramming.

**Open Data-Link Interface (ODI):** This is a protocol independent structure used by early Novel NetWare clients. It provides support for simultaneous connection to multiple network protocols.

**Open Entry:** A catalogue entry which provided for the addition of information covering a work of which the library does not have a complete set, or about which complete information is lacking. The chief use of open entries lies in the cataloguing of serial publications, for the inclusive dates of publication and the total number of volumes cannot be given until publication is complete or discontinued or the library discontinues adding part.

**Open Reel:** It is now rarely used for dissemination of copies of recordings, but it is still widely used for the preparation and storage of masters or orginals. While wider tapes are available for such purposes as studio recordings, the usual width of tape is 6.3 mm (¼ inch). The tape is supplied wound on a reel, the magnetic surface on the innerside, the reels are usually 8 cm, 13 cm, 18 cm or 26.5 mm (3 inch, 5 inch, 10-½ inch) in diameter.

**Open Source:** This is a software that can be freely distributed, and must be distributed along with the source code. Thus, the source can be changed easily and the programme can be altered to fix bugs or add features. Depending on the open source license, you may be unable to redistribute altered code, or charge money for the distribution of the software. Some popular examples of open source software are Linux and Netscape Communicator version 5 and greater.

**Operating System:** A set of system programme used to control input/output devices of a computer. Select appropriate software requested by users, allocate computer resources such as memory. CPU time and schedule user programmes.

**Operator:** (1) In symbol manipulation, a symbol that represents the action to be performed in an operation. (2) A person who operates a machine.

**Optical Disc:** Synonym for optical disk.

**Optical Disk:** A disk that will accept and retain data in the form of marks in a recording layer, that can be read with an optical beam. According to their function, optical disks are categorized in rewritable (with phase change or magneto-optical technology), write-once read many (magneto-optical technology), WORM (with phase change, ablative or other technology), read-only (embossed technology). Synonymous with optical disc, digital optical disk.

**Optical Scanner:** A scanner that uses optical processing for examining patterns.

**Optical Storage:** Storage in which data is placed and/or retrieved by means of a focused optical beam; for example, optical tape storage, optical disk storage, optical card storage. Optical techniques may also be combined with other techniques, such as in magneto-optical storage.

**Opus Number:** A number assigned to a work or a group of works, of a composer, generally indicating order of composition or a publication (ALA Gloss).

**Order Form File:** A copy of order form is kept in a file for office record in library. It is also used as checking document while books are received in the library.

**Order Form:** The form used for placing the order to the agency from where books are to be purchased. These forms have complete detail of the books and are signed by the purchase authority.

**Orissa Public Library Network:** It started in Second Five Year Plan. Orissa has no library network unlike the state of Tamil Nadu, Andhra Pradesh, Karnataka, and Maharashtra which have Public Library Act. Orissa has a State Library Advisory Board having a network of libraries. There is one State Central Library at Bhubneshwar, 15 District libraries, 18 sub-divisional libraries, 6 Ex-District Board libraries. It is managed by the department of Sports and Culture or Orissa State. There are 110 Municipal libraries-cum-reading rooms.

**O-ROM Disk:** A type of optical disk that provides for the whole of the disk surface to be pre-recorded, and reproduced by stamping or other means, for reading without recourse to the magneto-optical effect.

**Output Data:** (1) Data produced or to be produced by any component part of a computer. (2) Data that a data processing system, or any of its parts, transfers outside of that system or part.

**Output:** Anything that comes out of a computer or system. As in, "Watch out for that pile of OUTPUT on the sidewalk".

**Overflow:** (1) A condition that arises when the result of an operation exceeds the capacity of the numeration system used in a digital computer. (2) That portion of a word expressing the result of an arithmetic operation by which its word length exceeds the storage capacity of the intended storage device. (3) In calculators, the state in which the calculator is unable to accept or process the number of digits in the entry or the result.

**Overflow:** It is a situation when there is more information than can be handled. Often used to describe the production of a number larger than a variable can handle. For instance, if you are expecting 10 digits but receive 20.

**Overhead Bit**: An ancillary bit used for control purposes. Overhead bits are mainly used when the sending equipment carries out a process, particularly and a periodic process, to ensure that the receiving equipment carries out the corresponding complementary process. They are normally added at regular intervals to a digital signal at the sending end and removed at the receiving end. Synonymous with service bit.

***Oxford English Dictionary***: Philological Society, Oxford, Clarendon Press, 1933 (reprinted and revised continuously). It provides vocabulary, classification vocabulary on a large measure of dialected usage and slangs. It is in English language.

# P

**PAC:** Public Access Catalog. The SDSU University Library's online catalog which lists the books held here and the journals subscribed to but not their contents. It also provides information on circulation status, books and journals ordered but not yet received, receipt of journal issues, and more.

**Page Headline:** The chapter head or caption printed at the top of a page as an indication of the contents.

**Page Reference:** In book indexes, bibliographies, printed book catalogues, etc. the number of the page on which an article, word or entry indexed is to be found in a particular volume.

**Pagination:** The consecutive numbering of the pages of a book. Normal practice is for preliminary matter to be paged in Roman and for the text to be paged in Arabic numerals. In catalogue entry that part of the collection, which states the number of pages in the book.

**Palmtop:** This refers to a form factor of a computer that can easily fit in your palm. This usually refers to very small PDS's with no keyboards but can also refer to larger fold open PDS's, or micro laptops with full keyboards.

**Pamphlet:** (1) In a restricted technical sense, an independent publication consisting of new leaves of printed matter stitched together by not bound, usually enclosed in paper covers. (2) A brief controversial treatise on a topic of current interest, usually religious or political, common in England from the 16th to 18th century. (ALA Gloss).

**Parallel Computer:** A computer that has multiple arithmetic and logic units that are used to accomplish parallel operations or parallel processing. Contrast with serial computer.

**Parallel Transmission**: The simultaneous transmission over separate transmission channels of the signal elements of a group representing a character or other entity of data.

**Parity Memory**: Not quite memory that has a twin, but instead, more like a summary. The parity does not exactly have a copy of the original, but rather enough information to verify the integrity of the original.

**Partial Bibliography**: A bibliography compiled within some arbitrary limitation, perhaps limited to periodicals only, or books on one subject limited to a certain country or period of time, etc. but within the stated limitation as complete as possible.

**Partial Contents Note**: A note following the collation of a catalogue entry, listing only the more important items in the book.

**Partial Title**: A catch title consisting of only a part of the title as given on the title-page. It may be a secondary part of the title, as subtitle, or alternative title, or the title with the less significant words omitted.

**Partially Connected Network**: In artificial neural networks, a nonlayered network in which each artificial neuron is not necessarily connected to all the others, or a layered network in which each artificial neuron in a layer is not necessarily connected to all neurons in the adjacent forward layer.

**Pascal**: A high level programming language named after Blaise, Pascal. Used for a variety of applications, particularly suitable for non-numerical programming.

**Pascal**: This is a programming language that was designed to teach computer science students the concepts of programming. It is almost like C for dummies. In fact, the two languages are very similar, but the stoic brackets of C are changed to happy and fluffy "Begin" and "End" statements. Also, many of the more complex functions of Care missing, but it's still a fully functional language. Borland uses Pascal as the basis for its Delphi programming language.

**Peer-to-peer Network**: A computer network that contains only equivalent nodes with respect to their capability of control or operation.

**Periodical Circulation**: In practice, periodicals are not circulated. But a few libraries issue loose numbers to teachers till one volume is completed. There are many circulation methods applied in various libraries, i.e. routine slip method, group routine method, multiple periodical issue method, departmental issue method.

**Periodical**: A publication issued at regular or irregular interval each issue normally being numbered consecutively, distinguished from other serials in that the process of publication is continuous with no predetermined termination.

**Peripheral Equipment**: Any device that is controlled by and can communicate with a computer, for example, input/output units, external storage.

**Personal Administration**: Personal administration is concerned with library people and administration, which means responsibilities for accomplishment. It is a staff function.

**Personal Bibliography**: A bibliography of the persons, irrespective of their fields of activities from birth to death, literature divided into periods and phases of life. Sometimes, much of this literature may consist of diaries, memories and letters.

**Personal Computer (PC)**: A microcomputer primarily intended for stand-alone use by an individual.

**Personality**: A category of substantives which are unanalysable and have to be handled gently and as a whole.

**Phase Relation**: Complex subjects, having relation of various types are emerging day by day at a proliferating rate to the library. This relation may be between the basic classes, between the isolates of a facet and between sub-isolates of an isolate. Colon classification has made provision for phase relation. There are three levels of phase relation—inter subject, intra facet and intra array.

**Physical Schema:** The part of the database schema that pertains to the physical level.

**Place of Publication:** (1) The business address of the publishing house that issues the book. (2) As normally used in the imprint of a catalogue entry, the city or town in which the publishing house is located.

**Pocket (book):** A method of recording loans which is used in most public lending libraries. The books on the shelves contain a small pocket which holds a card carrying details of the book, readers are supplied with tickets which are in the form of a pocket so that, when a book is borrowed, the book card is transferred from the book packer to the reader's ticket.

**Point-to-point Protocol (PPP):** The protocol for transmitting network layer datagrams (such as IP packets) over serial point-to-point links via dial-up telephone. PPP provides greater protection for data integrity and security than does SLIP, but with greater overhead. Contrast with Serial Line Internet Protocol.

**Popsi:** The developed form of chain procedure is known as POPSI. It was developed by G. Bhattacharya and A. Neelameghan of DRTC Bangalore. This is postulates-based Permuted-Subject Indexing and procedure for implementing the policy 'grouping by juxtraposition' by keeping the structure of each specific subject heading parallel horizontally presented chain surviving as the basis. In other words POPSI is made from facet analysis. The subject of a document is to be face analysed according to the method.

**Port:** (1) To make the programming changes necessary to allow a programme that runs on one type of computer to run on another type of computer. (2) A termination point through which signals can enter or leave a network. (3) In a network, a functional unit through which data can enter or leave a network. (4) A physical or logical access point for data to enter or exit; for example, a physical point of connection into a computer or data network a logical access point at a host computer in an intranet. Synonymous with input/output port.

**Portability**: The capability of a programme to be executed on various types of data processing systems with little or no modification and without converting the programme into a different long.

**Portable Computer**: A microcomputer that can be hand-carried for use in more than one location.

**Portal**: A starting location on a network that provides access to predefined operations.

**Positional Notation**: A numeration system in which a number is represented by an ordered set of digits in such a way that the value contributed by a digit depends upon its position as well as upon its value. Synonymous with positional numeration system.

**PRECIS:** Derek Austin has developed new indexing system known as PRECIS (Pre Served Context Indexing System). It is computer-oriented system and is being used in British National Bibliography since 1971. There is sufficient provision of necessary subject reference index.

**Preface**: A brief discourse, or note, most frequently by the author of the book, preceding the text, normally explaining the purpose of the author in writing the book, its plan and development, often indicating the class of reader for whom the book is intended, and acknowledging the assistance received. Sometimes a preface may be considered as important as the text, as in the case of prefaces of George Bernard Shaw to his plays.

**Pre-Natal Cataloguing**: A term coined by S.R. Ranganathan and elaborated in his Heading and Canons: Comparative study of five catalogue codes, 1955 covering (a) the cataloguing of a book by a centralized cataloguing agency from a form copy of the book supplied pre-publication by the publisher so that catalogue cards are available on the day of publication and may be ordered by means of a reference number appearing in the book.

**Press Clippings**: The press cuttings or clippings are pasted on thicker sheet for easy handling and arranged in systematic order. Clippings constitute a course of information supplementing the general reference materials. News summaries are also covered by some current news indexes.

**Printer:** An output unit to print the result of computation. Line printer prints one full line at a time using a character, chain or drum. Character printers print one character at a time serially.

**Processor:** A unit of computer which interprets instructions, executes them using arithmetic and logic circuits and controls the operation of all the other units of the computer (Known as CPU).

**Programming Language:** An artificial language for expressing programmes.

**Programming System:** In a programming environment, the programming languages and software tools required for the development and use of programmes expressed in these programming languages.

**Prolog:** A fifth-generation programming language that allows coding of precise facts and rules; it uses a declarative instead of a procedural approach making the programmer describe what must be computed instead of how to perform the work. Prologue then organizes how the computations are to be earned out. It is primarily used for applications in artificial intelligence and in the development of expert systems. The name is derived from programming logic.

**PROM:** A storage device that, after being written on once, becomes a read-only memory, PROM is the abbreviation for programmable read-only memory.

**Protocol:** (1) A set of rules that determines the behaviour of functional units in achieving communication. (2) In programming languages, the set of rules that determines the behaviour of objects in the exchange of messages. (3) In OSI, a set of semantic and syntactic rules that determine the behaviour of entities in the same layer in performing communication functions.

**Public Library System in Manipur:** Manipur is the smallest state of India and situated in the north east of India. This state emerged in 1971. Manipur Library Association was rejuvenated on 24 May 1987. Public Library Bill was introduced in Manipur Legislative Assembly in July 1988, passed in Aug. 1988, and implemented in Aug. 1993. There is provision of Department of Public Library Committee, District Library Authority.

**Public Packet-Switched Data Network**: The Department of Telecommunication (DOT) has established this year, a nationwide public packet switched data network (PSDN) called I-Net. Initially I-Net will have nodes in cities connected through high speed (9600 and 64000 bytes per second) lines. I-Net support CCITT standard protocol/ interfaces: X.3, X.28, X.29, X.25, X.75. I-Net provides international connectivity to important data networks outside the country through GPSS (Gateway Packet Switched Service) of the VSNL, Indian overseas communication service at Bombay, Madras and Delhi.

**Punch Cards Charging**: It has been used for many years in the American IBM circulation control. The use of punched cards for charging is most likely to be economical where the sorting machines are already in use in another department of library authority. Free librarians have made a limited use of punched cards at transaction cards in conjunction with photo-charging. Although sorting by machine under these circumstances has obvious advantages over hand sorting.

**Push Technology**: In networking, a technique used to enable an Internet user to automatically get information in the future, based upon established criteria.

# R

**Radhakrishnan Commission, 1948**: The Indian Universities Education Commission was under the chairmanship of Dr. S.K. Radhakrishnan noted that library is a heart of all universities. It stressed for qualified library staff and keeping the library up-to-date.

**Raza Library (Rampur)**: Rampur Raza Library was established by Late Syed Faizulla Khan (d.1794), Nawab of Rampur and successfully patronised by his successors. Building was constructed in 1889. Nawab Sayed Raza Ali attached a press to the library for publication. The library published catalogue of Arabic manuscripts in 6 volumes and Urdu catalogue in one volume. In 1947 Govt. of Uttar Pradesh took over this library. Now it is under Government of India. There are 14,000 manuscripts in nine languages, 6,000 in Arabic, 6,000 in Persian, 1,500 in Urdu, 500 in Hindi, 100 photographs and 56,000 books.

**Raja Ram Mohan Roy Library Foundation**: The Ministry of Education and Culture, Govt. of India established an independent organization known as Raja Ram Mohan Roy Library Foundation in 1972 with a view to promote or support public library services movement in the country by providing adequate library services both in Urban and rural areas and by developing reading habits all over the country.

**Raleigh Commission, 1902**: Indian University Commission appointed by Lord Curzon under the Chairmanship of Sir Thomas Raleigh in 1902 noted the lack of library facilities in the universities and colleges and recommended good reference libraries.

**RAM**: (Random Access Memory) The memory used as main memory of a computer in which the time to retrieve stored information is independent of an address where it is stored.

**RAM**: Literally, any memory that can be addressed randomly. Note, however, that the term RAM is typically used to mean read/write memory as distinct from ROM which is read-only memory. RAM is the abbreviation for random access memory.

**Random Number**: (1) A number obtained by chance. (2) A number selected from a known set of numbers in such a way that each number in the set has the same probability of occurrence.

**Random Scan Display**: Also known as Vector display or calligraphic display. The display images by breaking them up into points, lines and segments of standard curves. The image is refreshed.

**Ranganathan Commission, 1957**: This Committee was formed to advise the University Grants Commission about the development of libraries on matters relating to the proper functioning and management of libraries.

**Ranganathan Library Review Committee 1965**: University Grants Commission appointed a Review Committee under the Chairmanship of Dr. S.R. Ranganathan and made recommendations on minimum qualification for admission in library science courses, staff requirement, minimum qualification of teachers, books, research and training for teachers.

**Raster Scan**: A plotter that generates a display image on a display surface using a line-by-line scanning technique.

**Read Only Memory (ROM)**: A storage device in which data under normal conditions, can only be read.

**Read/Write Memory**: A storage device in which data can be written and read.

**Read/Write Slot**: An operating slot in the jacket of a floppy disk to allow access to the tracks by the read/write heads. Synonymous with read/write opening.

**Reading List:** A list of books recommended for reading on a particular subject, often selected to fit the needs of a particular class of readers and possibly offering particulars of the purpose, scope and special features of each book. The arrangement of such lists is frequently alphabetical but suited to the study of the subject or for the class of reader.

**Real Time System:** A system in which a computer is used to control a physical system operating independently. The time taken to compute should match the needs of the physical system.

**Real-time Environment:** An operating environment that supports the execution of real-time programmes.

**Regional Computer Centres:** The Department of Electronics has been promoting appropriate computerization thoughtout Regional Computer Centres besides NIC and NCSDCT. The Regional Computer Centre, Calcutta has Borrowed B6738 computer system commissioned in 1977, and about 2000 individual and 250 organisations are using this centre, RCC of Chandigarh was established in 1979 and equipped with DEC2050 computer system.

**Relative Index:** A term used in classification to denote an index that lists a subject and also all related aspects of the subject that may appear elsewhere in the schedules.

**Remainder:** A publisher's stock of unsold copies of a book disposed of a lot, to be resold at a reduced price, also applied to the individual book sold under this arrangement.

**Remote System:** Another computer on the Internet to which you connect. Interactions between computers are often described using the terms "local" and "remote" systems. The local system is your computer and the remote system is the other computer.

**Removal Slip:** A card inserted in a catalogue to indicate that an entry has been removed temporarily for alternation. It bears sufficient information for the book to be identified, and indicates the whereabouts of the permanent card (Lib. Gloss).

**Renewal**: (1) The re-issue of a book to the same borrower for a further loan period. (2) The re-registration of a reader at the end of the period of library membership.

**Repairing**: The partial rehabilitation of a wornout binding including such operations as restoring cover and reinforcing at joints. Not to be confused with mending.

**Replacement**: (1) The substitution of another copy o a title or volume for one no longer in a library. (2) The copy of a title or volume substituted, or to be substituted, for another copy no longer in the library (ALA Gloss).

**Reprint Series**: A number of publications, being reprints, do not necessarily relate in subject or treatment, issued by a publisher in uniform style and are assigned a collective series title, for example, the *Everyman's Library* and *Collins' Classics*.

**Reprint**: Another printing of a work from the same standing type as the original or from a stereotype taken from the original. A new title-page may be substituted and corrections of minor errors in the text made, but the text remains substantially identical with the first printing. Where extensive revision of the text is made or the type is recomposed, the new printing must strictly be termed a new edition.

**Republication**: (1) A re-issuing of a work by a different publisher without change in text. Sometimes applied to a reprinting in another country. (2) In a very broad sense, a re-issuing of a work, with or without change in text, or as a new edition (ALA Gloss).

**Resampling**: An increase or reduction in the number of pixels in an image, required to change its resolution without altering its size. See also down-sampling and interpolation.

**Reserved Book**: A book which has been requested by a borrower usually by completing a notification form is intercepted at the return counter and the intending borrower is informed by post that the required book will be kept for a stated period. Libraries which arrange loan records in book order intercept by inserting a 'stop' signal in the loan record or 'charge'. Other libraries check all returned books against a visible index of those required.

**Resource-based Access Control:** In computer security, access control based on the subject's presentation of evidence of authorization, such as an object-related password, with a request for access to an object. Contrast with identity-based access control.

**Response Time:** The elapsed time between the end of a request to a data processing system and the beginning of the response; for example, the length of time between an indication of the end of an inquiry and the display of the first character of the response at a user terminal.

**Response Window:** Synonym for response time window.

**Retrieval function:** In a data manipulation language, a capability to select and to locate stored records with specified characteristics and to transfer these records to a working space for any required further processing by application software.

**Retrieval:** (1) In information processing, the act or process of recovering data or information. (2) In a conceptual schema language, the making known of sentence that has been inserted into the information base or conceptual schema, or that is deducible from other sentences in the information base or conceptual schema. (3) In electronic mail, a transmittal step in which a message or report is extracted from the user's message store and conveyed to the user's user agent. This user is an actual recipient.

**Revised Edition:** A new edition with the text of the original edition changed and corrected, and sometimes with additions that supplement it or bring it upto date (ALA Gloss).

**Rewritable Optical Disk:** An optical disk in which the data in specified areas can be rewritten by an optical beam.

RFC **(Request for Comments):** The name of the result and the process for creating a standard on the Internet. New standards are proposed and published on the Internet, as a Request For Comments. The proposal is reviewed by the Internet Engineering Task Force, a consensus-building body that facilitates discussion, and eventually a new standard is established, but the reference number/name for the standard retains the acronym RFC, e.g. the official standard for e-mail message formats is RFC 822.

**Robot System**: A manufacturing cell, including the robot hardware and software, consisting of the manipulator, the power supply, the control system, the end effectors, and including any equipment with which the robot is interfacing and any communications interface that is operating and monitoring the robot.

**Robot**: (1) A usually programmable mechanical device designed to perform tasks of manipulation or locomotion under automatic control. (2) The software analogue of a mechanical robot that can move around a network, sometimes called a bot, for example, a knowledge robot.

**ROM**: Read only memory. A memory in which information is permanently written. The information can be read quickly but not changed which steers messages through multiple LANS and ensures that the least congested route is taken by messages.

**ROM**: Read-Only Memory. It's like software that's hard-wired into your computer—basic, permanent information that tells it things like how to load up the operating system when you turn it on.

**Round**: In a compound focus, each fundamental catalogue may manifest more than one. Each such manifestation is a round. Further work is the classification of subjects of great intention leading to the recognition of the cycle of recurrence of the manifestations of the fundamental categories in compound subjects. This led to the postulates of rounds for personality, matter, and energy.

**Rule-based System**: A computer system that applies if-then rules to expressions to produce new expressions. In artificial intelligence, the expressions may be propositions. Synonymous with production system.

# S

**Sadlar Commission, 1917**: Calcutta University Commission appointed in 1917 under the Chairmanship of Dr. Michad Sadlar. He commented in his report under the heading 'The Neglect of Library' that libraries are badly neglected, librarian should be given a good status, such as the University librarian should be appointed executive councellor and ex-officio member of Academic Council.

**Sample Pages**: Selected specimen pages of a book printed to indicate to prospective purchasers the style of the forthcoming volume.

**Save Area**: In the context of temporary transfer of control from one programme to another, an area of storage in which the registers and process data of the first programme are stored so that the first programme can be reactivated; this is applicable, for example, to multiprogramming, interrupt handling, and library calls.

**Saymour Lubetzky**: He worked on ALA rules and expressed his view in his "Cataloguing rules and principles: a critique of the ALA rules for entry and a proposed design for their revision" published in 1953. In 1956, Lubetzky was appointed editor to prepare a new code.

**Scalar Type**: A data type, each instance of which represents a scalar. Pascal simple types are either ordinal types or real types. Ada scalar types are either discrete types or real types. Synonymous with simple type.

**Scalar**: A quantity characterized by a single value. Contrast with vector.

**Scale**: (1) To alter the manner in which values are represented so as to bring them into a different range, for example, to change inches to centimeters. (2) In computer graphics, to enlarge or diminish all or part of a display image. Scaling does not have to be carried out with the same scale factor in all directions.

**Scan**: (1) To systematically examine data. (2) To use a scanner. (3) In computer vision, to examine an object or synthesize an image according to a predetermined sequence. Graphic images may be generated by a faster scan system. Examples:

(a) A fax system scanning a subject image left to right and top to bottom, as when reading;

(b) Reader scanning from the image centre outward at various angles corresponding to compass directions;

(c) Generation of a television picture, line by line.

**Scanner**: (1) A device that examines text, images, or patterns, and generates signals corresponding them. (2) In computer vision, a vision sensor that scans its environment in a systematic pattern; for example, a device that optically scans printed or written data and generates their digital representations.

**Schema**: (1) In artificial intelligence, a formalism for representing information about a simple concept, an entity, or a class of objects by means of its possible uses. The schema shows ways of using a concept. It does not describe typical instances of that concept. (2) A complete description of the structure of a database pertaining to a specific level of consideration.

**Scientific Visualization**: The use of computer graphics and image processing to present models or characteristics of processes or objects for supporting human understanding, for example, a display image created by combining magnetic resonance scans of a tumor, and volumetric top and side views of a lake showing temperature data; a two-dimensional model of electrical waves in the heart. Synonymous with visualization (in computer graphics).

**Screen Editor**: A text editor that displays text on a screen and allows text editing of arbitrary character strings using cursor positions, without regard to line numbers.

**Screen Frequency**: The number of rows or lines of dots in a halftone image within a given distance, normally stated in lines per inch (lpi) or lines per centimeter (l/cm). A frequency of 200 lpi would only be used in high quality printing.

**Script Software**: Synonym for scriptwave.

**Script**: (1) A term applied to any type face resembling handwriting. (2) A typescript, specifically, a typescript of a play, or film play, the text of the spoken part of a radio programme, etc. (ALA Gloss).

**Script**: (1) In knowledge representation, an event-oriented knowledge representation that uses predetermined sequences of events to determine the results of interactions between known entities. The event is represented by means of scenes, settings, thematic roles, and props. (2) In hypermedia and multimedia, a specification of how hyperobjects are to be presented to a user and how input from the user is to be handled.

**Scriptware**: Software designed for the creation of scripts. Synonymous with script software.

**Scroll Bar**: A bar placed on any edge of a screen or a window, used to control scrolling or to indicate the position range of the data or display image currently displayed.

**Scrolling**: The movement of a display image vertically or horizontally, to view data not otherwise visible within the boundaries of a screen or window.

**Search and Replace**: A function or mode that enables a user to locate occurrences of such things as particular character strings, embedded commands, or characters with a specific attribute in text and selectively replace them with new text entered as part of the command. This function or mode may be performed on part of, or throughout, the document. Synonymous with find and replace.

**Search Time**: The time required for the read/write head of a direct access storage device to locate a particular record on a track corresponding to a given address or key. Search time is part of the latency, immediately following the seek time, and is followed by transfer time. Synonymous with rotational delay.

**Search**: (1) The examination of one or more data elements of a set to find those elements that have a given property. (2) In text processing, a function or mode that enables a user to locate occurrences of such things as particular character strings.

**Second Vertical**: The second vertical line from the left on a standard ruled catalogue card, making the position of 'second indentation'.

**Secondary Bibliography**: An 'intensive' or special bibliography dealing with books relating to one subject for the compilation of which primary bibliographics have been used (Lib. Gloss).

**See Copy**: An instruction to the printer to refer to the original manuscript to rectify an error.

**See Reference**: A direction in a catalogue from a term or name under which no entries are listed to the heading where entries are listed.

**Segmentation**: A technique for storage allocation in which parts of a programme are loaded from auxiliary storage into main storage when needed.

**Select List**: A reading list which includes a selection only of the books in the library on the subject of the list (Lib. Gloss).

**Selective Bibliography**: One which gives only a selection of the literature concerned, such selection having been made deliberately, either to meet the needs of a particular class of user or to exclude minor material, pamphlet material, etc. (See also electric bibliography).

**Self-Education**: Self-education starts at the point where the formal education ends. Education is a continuous process. Library provides self-education. Library services are being extended to the community even outside the four walls of a library building through the extension services, for example adult education, continuing education, etc.

**Self-learning:** Learning from an internal knowledge base, or from new input data, without introduction of explicit external knowledge.

**Shelf List:** A record of the books in a library arranged in the order in which they stand on the shelves. Although sometimes used as a subject catalogue of the library, for which purpose the lack of bibliographic detail and analysis and lack of cross-references limit its usefulness, its primary purpose is to serve as the official inventory of the library's stock. Shelf lists are often kept in the form of sheaf catalogues, and a successful system has been maintained on 3" × 2" cards. Shelf list is generally a copy of entry.

**Sensitive Information:** In security, information that, as determined by a competent authority, must be protected because its disclosure, modification, destruction, or loss will cause perceivable damage to someone or something.

**Serial Cable/Serial Port:** A cable used to connect peripheral devices through a computer's script port. Normally a 25-pin connector on each end, yet can be a 9-pin on one. A Serial Port can either be plugged into an expansion slot on the motherboard of your computer or built into the motherboard itself. Serial ports are used for such devices as printers, mice, and moderns.

**Serial Catalogue:** A public or an official catalogue of serials in a library, with a record of the library's holdings (ALA Gloss).

**Serial Control:** Serial control area involves three areas—acquisition control, bibliographical control, inventory control.

**Serial Number:** (1) The number denoting the place of the publication in a series (A.A. Code). (2) One of the consecutive numbers sometimes assigned to entries in a bibliography or a printed catalogue. (3) A card number.

**Series Entry:** (1) In a bibliography, a complete or partial list of the works published in a series listed under the name of the series. (2) A catalogue entry, made under the name of the series as heading, listing briefly the several works in the library which belong to that series.

**Series Note**: A note in a catalogue entry, ordinarily following the collation, starting (usually in parentheses) the name of the series to which the book belongs.

**Series Title**: The name of the series to which a book belongs, indicated on the cover, title paper or somewhere else in the book.

**Server**: A computer, or a software package, that provides a specific kind of service to client software running on other computers. The term can refer to a particular piece of software, such as a WWW server, or to the machine on which the software is running, e.g. "Our mail server is down today, that's why e-mail isn't getting out".

**Shell**: (1) An empty expert system structure into which a particular field of expertise is built. Synonymous with expert system shell. (2) A software interface between a user and the operating system of a computer. Shell programmes interpret commands and use interactions on devices such as keyboards, pointing devices, and touch-sensitive screens and communicate them to the operating system. Shells simplify user interactions by eliminating the user's concern with operating system requirements. A computer may have several layers of shells for various levels of user interaction. (3) Software that allows a kernel to run under different operating system environments.

**Short-form Cataloguing**: That kind of cataloguing in which, as a matter of policy, the entries give only the briefest possible details consistent with recognition of each item.

**Signature**: (1) The observable or characteristic measurement or feature pattern derived from entities of a particular category; for example, the feature pattern that determines the particular class of entities. (2) In electronic mail, at the end of the body, a specific piece of text designed by the originator for individual identification. The signature usually contains name, address, and may also include telephone and fax numbers. The signature may include a digital signature or other data authenticating the message.

**Silk Screen:** A stencil process for multiplying an original design and lettering in colours which is frequently used for posters and other jobs requiring short runs and for which lithography would be too expensive. Bolting silk, organdie, phosphor bronze or steel gauze are tightly stretched over a wooden frame. A stencil bearing the design is fixed to the underside of the silk or other material and the paint is forced through the silk at the open parts of the stencil with a rubber squeegee on to the paper, silk, metal, glass, wood, or other material to be printed (Lib. Gloss).

**Silking:** A means of repairing or preserving paper by the application of silk chiffon to one or both sides of the paper.

**Silverfish:** A small silvery-white hexapod resembling the centipede which feeds on the starchy filter of paper, cloth and paste, and is highly destructive to paper. It seems to favour dampness and is found most often where dampness and mildew are present (Book Gloss).

**Simulate:** To represent certain features of the behaviour of a physical or abstract system by the behaviour of another system, for example, to represent a physical phenomenon by means of operations performed by a computer or to represent the operations of a computer by those of another computer. Contrast with emulate.

**Single-layered Network:** In artificial neural networks, a layered network having only source nodes and one output layer, without hidden layers. In a single-layered network, only the output layer performs computation.

**Sinha Committee, 1955:** Govt. of India appointed an advisory committee under the chairmanship of Shri K.P. Sinha. It recommended free library service to the citizens of India. Every Panchayat should have a library. There should be an All India Library Council at National, State level. Library co-operation should be strengthened and librarian should be equated with teachers.

**Sir Anthony Panizzi:** A great cataloguer who followed the Anglo-American traditions. He was Assistant Librarian in British Museum Library in 1831, Keeper of Printed Books in 1932.

He formulated 91 rules to govern the compilation of printed book catalogues.

**Slides**: Slides are mounted on storage cases. The mounts can be cardboard or plastic. Glass is sometimes used to cover and protect the film within the mount. They are placed in a slide box with sets numbered serially. It has two two-common formats (a) 35 mm (b) 110 mm format. There is also a 60 mm square slide which can be mounted and used in major lectures. The dimensions of a slide may be increased to 250 mm square.

**Smart Card**: A credit card type electronic card that contains a microprocessor programmed to perform several functions when used at a suitable terminal. Examples of these functions are communications, identification, medical records, and electronic banking. Synonymous with chip card.

**Soft Hyphen**: A special character in a word, inserted automatically or by the user to mark where the word can be divided, and displayed as a hyphen when the word must be divided at the end of the line due to lack of space. Soft hyphens are subject to hyphen drop. Synonyınous with discretionary hyphen. Contrast with hard hyphen.

**Software Library**: In programming, a controlled collection of software and related documentation designed to aid in software development, use, or maintenance.

**Software Package**: A complete and documented set of programmes supplied to several users for a generic application or function. Some software packages are alterable for a specific application.

**Software**: All or part of the programmes, procedures, rules, and associated documentation of a data processing system or an information processing system. Software is an intellectual creation that is independent of the medium on which it is recorded. Contrast with hardware.

**Source Index**: A card index to sources of unusual and elusive information, which, in addition to listing publications, may refer to individuals and organizations. More common in special libraries (ALA Gloss).

**Space:** (1) In text processing, a basic unit of area, usually the size of a single character. (2) One or more space characters. (3) In text processing, to advance, physically or logically, the print or display position according to a prescribed format. For example, to advance the print or display position horizontally to the right or vertically downward.

**Special Purpose Computer:** A computer that is designed to operate upon a restricted class of problems.

**Special-purpose Language:** A programming language that focuses its capabilities on a particular kind of application, for example, a form-filling language. Also postscript.

**Specification Language:** A problem-oriented language, often a computer-processible combination of natural language and artificial language, used for expressing the requirements, design, behaviour, or other characteristics of a system or a component and that provides special language constructs and, sometimes, verification protocols used to develop, analyze, and document the specified entities.

**Speech Bandwidth:** The range of speech frequencies that can be transmitted or recorded by a given system.

**Speech Clipping:** The limiting of peak signals to a maximum amplitude value.

**Splash Screen:** A temporary screen or window displayed by a computer to inform, warn, or alert the viewer that a significant event has happened or is about to happen. Splash screens are used to inform, to warm, or to alert the user of errors or to offer a choice for some system option or to advertise a product or to inform the user of progress in a process such as programme installation.

**Splitting:** In electronic mail, a transmittal event in which message transfer agent replicates a message or probe, in order to convey each new instance in the transmittal step to its immediate recipients in a different manner.

**Standards:** Standards are documents formulated by agreement, authority or custom of sponsors, to define product, material, process or procedure, quality, construction, operating characteristics, performance nomenclature and other life facts, standards could be qualitative and quantitative.

**Statement:** (1) An explicitly terminated syntactic unit either representing a declaration or prescribing a unit of work that includes identification of actions to be performed, operands (if any) to be used in performing these actions, and disposition of any results. Some programming languages do not consider declarations to be statements. (2) Deprecated synonym for instruction.

**Stereoscopic System:** An imaging system designed to produce spatial impression by displaying different images to each eye. Examples are: (1) Anaglyphic, in which complementary coloured lenses cause each eye to see only one image of the pair; (2) Split screen, in which optical means are used to separate the two interleaved images for each eye; 3. Dual, screens, which use video displays to present different images simultaneously.

**Stigmonym:** They use of dots in a book as a substitute for the name of the author, a form of pseudonym. Where the author's name cannot be identified, such books as are published under stigmonym are catalogued under their titles.

**Stored Message Summary Service:** A service that provides a recipient's user agent with a count of the number of messages satisfying a specified criterion based on one or more attributes of the message stored in the message store.

**Stroke Device:** An input unit that provides a set of coordinates for recording a path of the unit. For example, an input unit that returns a polyline or cursor positions entered with the physical locator. Many physical devices such as locators, valuator devices, choice devices, may be simulated in graphics and thus become logical input units.

**Subheading:** A second, or a later part of a subject heading, added to divide the entries under a subject. Also a second part of an author heading for a corporate body, or the name of a ministry or government department following the name of a country (ALA Gloss).

For example:

Art-Bibliographies

Art Dictionaries

Art Essays

Art History

Great Britain. **Air Ministry**

Great Britain. **Board of Trade**

Great Britain. **Ministry of Works**

**Syntactic Analysis:** Most information analysis systems (Indexing) are based on the recognition of certain key elements. Often chosen from a pre-constructed list of acceptable items and on the determination of rules on which these basic elements are combined into larger units. The syntactical analysis identifies the roles of the word in the sentences, i.e. its grammatical class (i.e. part of speech) and relation among the words in sentence.

**Subject Analytical Entry**: An analytical entry in a catalogue for part of the work or for an article contained in a collection, made under the subject of the part or article analysed.

**Subject Bibliography**: A list of material about a given subject, whether the subject be a person, place or thing (ALA Gloss).

**Subject Card**: A catalogue card bearing a subject entry.

**Subject Catalogue**: (1) A catalogue consisting of subject entries only. (2) A loose term designing any catalogue arranged by subjects, whether alphabetical or classified. It relates one main subject or any of the divisions.

**Subject Cataloguing**: That phase of the process of cataloguing which concerns itself with the subject matter of books; hence, includes classification and the determination of subject headings (ALA Gloss).

**Subject Entry**: (1) An entry in a catalogue or a bibliography under a heading that indicates the subject of the work entered (ALA Gloss). (2) In an index, an entry relating to some subject or distinguished from one beginning with the name of a person (Lib. Gloss).

**Subject Heading**: A word or group of words expressing a subject, under which as heading, entries for all works on that subject are filled in a catalogue or bibliography.

**Subject Index**: These are those indexes which cover several periodicals. Very often there also includes new books, pamphlets, conference proceedings, reports, etc.

**Subject Series**: A number of books, ordinarily not reprints, dealing with different phases of a single subject or with a special field of literature, usually by different individual authors, uniform in textual and physical characteristics and published by a single publisher (ALA Gloss).

**Subject**: (1) In computer security, an active entity that can access objects, for example, a process that involves execution of a programme. A subject may cause information to flow among objects or may change the state of the data processing system. (2) In electronic mail, the part of a heading that summarizes the content of die message as specified by the originator.

**Subject-word Entry**: Entry under a word of the title indicative of the subjects, e.g. Archaeology, *Making a Start in*.

**Subscription Books**: (1) Those published at intervals by societies and issued to subscribing members. (2) Individual books of limited appeal, the publication of which depends to some extent on subscriptions promised prior to publication, and the price of which is raised after publication (Lib. Gloss).

**Substitution**: Encryption that replaces bit strings or character strings with other bit strings or character strings. The resulting ciphertext is called substitution cipher.

**Subsymbolic Representation**: A technique for knowledge representation that distributes the representation over a relatively large network rather than storing symbols directly. In the connectionist model, the knowledge stored in the network is inherent in the connection weights and cannot easily be expressed as simple rules or symbolic forms.

**Systematic Bibliography:** The enumeration and classification of books. The assembling of bibliographical entries into logical and useful arrangement for study and reference (Lib. Gloss).

**Systematic Catalogue:** A catalogue of subject entries, arranged in a logical order of subjects according to a systematic scheme of classification.

# T

**Tabulator:** A device that reads data from a data medium such as punched tape and produces lists, tables, or totals.

**TCP:** A connection-oriented protocol designed to provide a communications protocol used in the Internet. TCP provides a reliable host to protocol between hosts in packet-switched communications networks and in interconnected systems of such networks. TCP corresponds approximately to transport layer protocols within the OSI reference model. TCP is the abbreviation for Transmission Control Protocol.

**Teleconferencing:** Interactive communication among participants at different locations, using telecommunication facilities. Teleconferencing includes conference calls and video conferencing with still or moving images.

**Teleconferencing:** It is the technology responsible for human interaction via electronic networks. It is the most exciting development in human communications. Teleconferencing applied to conferencing of three or more persons at different location. Library and information professionals are not far behind in making use of teleconferencing. American Library Association has presented key sessions in 62 cities. It is becoming popular day by day.

**Telephone:** It is an answering machine for receiving and recording incoming calls. It has handset offering features such as memory for storing and dialing frequently used number and automatic redial. Telephone conferencing is possible so that served parties can be linked together in a single call.

**Teletex:** An enhanced version of telex that provides both upper and lower case transmission at higher speeds than telex.

**Teletext:** A broadcasting service that provides selectable text material such as news, weather reports,and advertisements, directly to a subscriber's television set. The subscriber must have a special decoder to receive teletext signals.

**Telex:** Telex is the most popular way of communicating text over the telephone network. Telex is transmitted and received by teletypewriter, which is a kind of communicating typewriter with a paper tape punch and readers' context between two teletypes is established by dialing in the usual way and the text is typed into the transmitting teletype by the telex operator. However, in order to save time on telephone line, the message will normally be recorded on paper tape before the call takes place. The receiving teletype is activated automatically on dial up and prints message.

**Telnet:** A virtual-terminal protocol that is used to remove terminal connection service and that allows a terminal at one site to interact with systems at other sites as if that terminal were directly connected to computers at those sites. There is also a specific protocol, called Telenet, that is defined for use with TCP/IP.

**Telnet:** It is used for logging in to other computers on the internet. It is used to access databases, library catalogue, etc. It is a software tool.

**Terminal Server:** A special purpose computer that has places to plug in many modems on one side, and a connection to a LAN or host machine on the other side.. Thus, the terminal server does the work of answering the calls and passes the connections on to the appropriate node. Most terminal servers can provide PPP or SLIP services if connected to the Internet.

**Text Editing:** Using a text processor to prepare or modify text, such as making additions or deletions, rearranging the text, or reformatting. Synonymous with editing.

**Text Processing:** Data processing operations on text such as entering, text editing, sorting, merging, retrieving, storing, displaying, or printing. Synonymous with word processing.

**Text Processor:** A software package or a device with associated software that enables a user to perform text processing. Synonymous with the word processor.

**Text:** (1) Data in the form of characters, symbols, words, phrases, paragraphs, sentences, tables, or other character arrangements, intended to convey a meaning, and whose interpretation is essentially based upon the reader's knowledge of some natural language or artificial language, for example, a business letter printed on paper or displayed on a screen. (2) In data communications, a sequence of characters treated as an entity, if preceded by one start-of-text character and terminated by one end-of-text character, respectively.

**Textual Bibliography:** It is a bibliography applied to textual studies. It deals with textual variations between a manuscript and then printed book or between various reprints or editions.

**Thermal Printer:** A nonimpact printer in which the characters or images are produced by applying hot elements to heat-sensitive paper directly or by melting ink from a ribbon onto plain paper.

**Thermal Wax Transfer:** A printing process using small heating elements to melt dots of wax pigment on a carrier film, which are then transferred to paper or transparent film by contact. This differs from the dye sublimation process in that individual dots do not fuse together, so thermal wax transfer appears to be of a lower resolution.

**Third Indention:** The distance from the left edge of a catalogue card at which, according of predetermined rules, certain parts of the description begin or continue. Generally the second indention is to the right of the first indention (ALA Gloss).

**TIFF:** Tag Image File Format. In a graphic file format, TIFF files are also bit maps, but they can be of any size, resolution, or color depth. It is the most versatile, reliable, and widely supported bit-mapped format and is the standard format for saving scanned images. However, the format does have several variations which means that occasionally an application may have trouble opening a TIFF file created by another programme.

**Time Isolate:** The term time isolate denotes millennium, century, decade, year and so on. Ranganathan decided Time Isolate in two categories—Public time and Featured time. Public time is represented by Roman capitals as the first significant digit. It is attached by a connecting symbol single inverted comma (') in the construction of the class number.

**Time Stud:** It is a tool of wage incentives system in a library. It determines the standard time required to carry out a job most efficiently. It is a method of finding out the one best way of doing the work in libraries. Time study is recorded on the basis of the time taken in completing the job cycle.

**Title Analytical Entry:** A catalogue entry for a part of a work, or for some article contained in a collection, made under the title of that part or article as heading, and including a reference to the publication in which the part of article appears.

**Title Entry:** An entry for a book in a catalogue or bibliography, made under a word of the book's title, usually the first word other than an article, or heading. In a catalogue the main entry of anonymous works, serial and periodical publications, encyclopaedia and the like will invariably be a title entry, whilst added entries under title are usually made for works of fiction, for individual short stories, plays, poems having distinctive titles, musical compositions, collections and composite works, pseudonymous works and for any work having a striking or fanciful title under which reference may be made by an enquirer.

**Title Page:** A page at the front of a book containing the full title and usually the name of the author, editor, translator, etc. the edition statement and the imprint. The term is often used wrongly to mean title leaf. In the case of works in oriental language the title-page and preliminary are normally found at the back of the volume.

**Token:** In a local area network, a specified group of bits serving as a symbol of authority passed successively from one data station to another to indicate the station temporarily in control of the transmission medium. All information is conveyed by frames. Some frames contain a token and no user data, others contain user data and no token.

**Token-bus Network:** A bus network in which a token passing protocol is used.

**Token-ring Network:** A ring network that allows unidirectional data transmission between data stations, by a token passing protocol, such that the transmitted data return to the originating station.

**Trade Bibliography:** A list of books in print or for sale, compiled by a publisher, a bookseller or a group of such agencies.

**Trade Catalogue:** (1) A book or pamphlet issued by a manufacture of a dealer, or by a group of manufacturers, illustrating and describing their products or goods and sometimes including, or accompanied by a price list. (2) A trade bibliography is trade list.

**Train of Characteristics:** A succession of characteristics used in subdividing a universe so as to yield in succession, the whole or not leading to organ or constituents.

**Transmission Channel:** A means of transmission of signals in one direction between two points. A transmission channel may be provided, for example, by frequency division multiplexing or time division multiplexing or time division multiplexing. Synonymous with channel.

**Tree Network:** A network in which there is exactly one path between any two nodes.

**Tree:** A data structure containing nodes that are linked together hierarchically with at the most one parent node for each node, and with only one root node.

# U

**Union Catalogue**: An author or a subject catalogue of all the books or selection of books, in a group of libraries, covering books in all fields or limited by subject or type of material, generally established by cooperative effort (ALA Gloss).

**Union Catalogue**: It is a catalogue listing in one sequence the holding or part of the holding of two or more libraries. Union Catalogue may be local, regional or national. Further division may be done on the basis of the kinds of material included, e.g. books, periodical, films, etc.

**Union Finding List**: A complete record of the holdings for a given group of libraries of material of a given type, in a certain field, or on a particular subject (ALA Gloss).

**Unisist**: UNESCO's International System of Scientific and Technological Information, Paris. It is a UNESCO programme launched in cooperation with American National Federation of Scientific Union and International Council of Scientific Union (ICSU). It works for improvement of the tools of system interconnection, effective implementation of information services, resources, development of structure and information policy and international distance to developing countries.

**Unit Card**: A catalogue card beating a main entry for a work which is used at a basic unit for all entries of that work in the catalogue. As many unit cards as are required to cover all entries are produced by printing or other means of duplication; one is filed intact as a main entry, appropriate headings being superimposed on the others which are then filed as added entries.

A catalogue composed of unit cards is economical in that mechanical reproduction of entries replaces individual typewriting or handwriting. It is efficient because every entry supplies full information and is less confusing for the lay enquirer since all entries appear in a standard form. Catalogue cards produced by centralized cataloguing agencies are usually unit cards and bear standard tracings at the foot of the entry.

**Universal Personal Telecommunications** (UPT): A service that:

(a) enables access to telecommunications services while accommodating personal mobility; and

(b) enables each user to participate in a user-defined set of subscriber services and to initiate and receive calls on the basis of a unique, personal, network-independent UPT Number across multiple networks at any terminal, fixed, movable, or mobile, regardless of geographic location.

Access to the service is limited only by terminal and network capabilities and restrictions imposed by the network provider. Contrast with personal communications services.

**Universal Bibliography**: A bibliography of the world's books. It provides wide, comprehensive and is not limited by time, place, language, subject authors or purpose.

**Universal Resource Locator (URL)**: A universal naming convention that is used for locating and accessing resources via the Internet. The general form of a URL is as follows: scheme://<user>:<password>@.<host-name>: <port>/ <path>/file

Some parts are not necessary in all cases.

**Unix**: Unix (officially trademarked as UNIX(®) is a computer operating system originally developed in 1969 by a group of AT&T employees at Bell Labs including Ken Thompson, Dennis Ritchie and Douglas McIlroy. Today's Unix systems and split into various branches, developed over time by AT&T as well as various commercial vendors and non-profit organiations.

**Unsupervised Learning**: A learning strategy that consists of observing and analyzing different entities and determining that some of their subsets can be grouped into certain classes, without any correctness test being performed on acquired knowledge through feedback from external knowledge sources. Once a concept is formed, it is given a name that may be used in subsequent learning of other concepts. Synonymous with learning without a teacher.

**Usenet**: A loosely connected set of computers and networks for creating, forwarding, or displaying computer conference based on the concept of distributed bulletin board systems.

**User Data Area**: On an optical disk, a part of the information zone containing user data. Synonymous with data zone.

**User Data**: (1) The data recorded on a data medium for a user as contrasted with data controlling the processing of such data. (2) In electronic mail, in HTML, or in other application software, the information to be transmitted from one user to one or more other users. Contrast with header. (3) In OSL data transferred between entities of a given layer on behalf of the entities of the next higher layer for which the former entities are providing services.

**User Friendly**: Pertaining to the ease and convenience of use by humans.

**User Manual**: A document that describes how to use a functional unit, and that may include description of the rights and responsibilities of the user, the owner, and the supplier of that functional unit. Synonymous with user's guide.

**User**: (1) A person, device, programme, or computer system that uses a computer system for the purpose of data processing and information exchange. (2) In electronic mail, a person or a functional unit that participates in message handling as a potential source or destination.

**Users**: Library clientele is a user, whosoever they may be, and of any caste or creed. Teachers, students, non-teaching staff in academic libraries, any person of society in public library or other persons of special fields in technical or special libraries are the users. Self-guiding, organizing orientation week, lecture method, library tour, audio-visual methods, and books are the methods and means for the users.

# V

**Video Conferencing**: Teleconferencing that provides transmission of still or moving images of participants, in addition to sound, text, and graphics.

**Video Signal Frame**: All the signals needed to produce a single image, for example, the 525 lines of standard NTSC Television.

**Video**: Data in a format suitable for a display as one or more images, for example, the content of a video cassette of a movie, or the signal from a weather radar. Video is usually presented as a series of images in a manner to give the impression of action or changing conditions.

**Videodisc**: A 12-inch disk that is similar to an audio CD but holds visual images (such as high-quality movies) as well as music. Also called a laserdisc.

**Video-Phones and Video Conferencing**: The video part of the unit consists of a black and white camera and monitor. Video conferencing systems are also available. This enables several callers to have meeting without needing to travel long distances.

**Videotex**: A service that provides interactive exchange of alphanumeric and graphics information over a telecommunication network. This information is displayed on a screen. Videotex or viewdata, are the terms used to describe computer based information systems such as organize the display text and graphics in the form of an electronic book. The information is held on frames or pages.

**Vidyanet**: It links several research institutions and laboratories, universities and higher educational institutions, research centres of industrial and other commercial organizations.

**Vinity:** (Moscow). It was established in 1952 and started service in 1953. It is known as 'Vsesanznyi Institute Manchoi Teagri Mecheskoi' (in Russian) and 'All Union Institute of Scientific and Technical Information (in English) under the USSR State Council for Coordination of Scientific Research Department (GKKNIR). It works for organization of information, processing of information, aid to research, and mechanical retrieval. It covers reviews, popular news, fanciful title, monographs, books, reference documents, textbooks, pamphlets, dissertations and other research material. It subscribes periodicals of 117 countries in 65 language. Its budget is 4-5% of National Abstracting Service which includes 25000 subject specialists, 20000 journals scanned, 1 lakh articles abstracting. It is publishing 'Express information' in 61 series and the Zhurnal Abstract. VINITY run, specialized training courses.

**Virtual Disk:** A portion of a physical disk that certains virtual machine operating systems can access as if it were logically a separate disk.

**Virtual File:** A selected set of data objects, such as in a database management system, that is accessed as if it were a separate file.

**Virtual Machine:** A computer as it is available to a user which is not merely the hardware but the hardware made usable by an operating system software, high level language and application programmes.

**Virtual Memory (VM):** A storage implementation that extends the apparent size of memory by using a large address space that is dynamically mapped into real memory addresses, and by swapping data from external storage into memory as required.

**Virtual:** Pertaining to something that appears to have some characteristics of something else for which it serves as a surrogate.

**Virus Signature:** A unique bit string that is common to each copy of a particular virus and that may be used by a scanning programme to detect the presence of the virus.

**Virus**: A programme that propagates itself by modifying other programmes to include a possibly changed copy of itself and that is executed when the infected programme is invoked. A virus often causes damage or annoyance and may be triggered by some event such as the occurrence of a predetermined date.

**Visible Index**: (1) A series of metal frames or panels for holding card records so that a group of cards can be seen at one time. Also called 'visible file'. (2) A record kept in such a device, as a list of serials, with or without bolsings (ALA Gloss).

**Visual Memory**: A hierarchy of a fast main memory and a slower peripheral memory managed by a software system in such a way that the user has an effective addressable memory which equals the sum of capacities of the two memories with an access time approaching that of fasting memory.

**Vocabulary-independent Recognizer**: A speech recognizer that is not limited to a list of words or sentences defined previously or given online. Synonymous with vocabulary-independent recognition system.

**Vocoder**: A speech coding device that extracts speech signal parameters that allow the intelligible recostruction of the initial speech signal. Synonymous with voice coder.

**Voice Control System**: A system in which a speech recognizer issues commands to computer-controlled equipment in response to speech input, for example, a robot that responds to simple spoken commands for movement. Synonymous with voice controller.

**Volume Number**: (1) A number assigned to a volume of a serial, a set or a series, (2) A number added to a book number to distinguish one volume from another of the same work (ALA Gloss).

**Voluminous Author**: A term adopted by cataloguers to describe an author under whose name many titles are entered, often extended to include also persons who are the subject of many biographies and the like. Voluminous authors pose the problem of sub-arranging the numerous entries under one heading, the most generally used basic arrangement being as follows:

1. Collected works;
2. Selections;
3. Single works in alphabetical order of title or uniform title.

Standard catalogue arrangement in detail for such authors are provided in the Anglo-American Code (for bible). Sear's list of subject headings (for Shakespeare), Library of Congress Subject headings..... (for Shakespeare, George Washington, etc.)

**VRAM**: Video RAM. A type of memory dedicated to handling the image displayed on a monitor. VRAM is built into many Macs, and it also comes on display cards.

**VRML**: A standardized modeling language for describing a three-dimensional virtual world that can be viewed and manipulated interactively. VRML is the abbreviation for Virtual Reality Modeling Language.

# W

**WAN**: Wide area network.

**Web Browser**: Also known as Web client programme, this software allows you to access and view HTML documents. Netscape, Mosaic, Lynx, Win Web, and Mac Web are some examples of Web browsers.

**Web Page**: A document that conforms to the rules of the World Wide Web. Usually, the frame of the Web page written in HTML, but its subparts may be in other notations.

**Web Server**: A server that provides access to files or other applications for the users of the World Wide Web. The protocol for communication between a Web server and a client is usually HTTP.

**Web**: WWW (World Wide Web)

**Webmaster**: The person responsible for managing and maintaining a Web server.

**Weeding of Books**: Libraries weed out the unused and obsolete books to save space, to give easy access to the collection and to give impressive look to the collection to attract the users. Weeding should be a regular process and carried out in a planned manner. Libraries weed out their collection after a proper scrutiny by the proper authority or the committee constituted for the purpose.

**Wide Area Information Server**: WAIS.

**Wide Area Network (WAN)**: A network that provides communication services to a geographic area larger than that served by a local area network or a metropolitan area network.

**Widow:** A last line of a paragraph that is carried over to the top of the next column or page, where it stands alone. Synonymous with widow line. Contrast with orphan.

**Window RAM (WRAM):** A type of RAM providing excellent graphics and floating-point performance.

**Window:** (1) A part of a display image with defined boundaries in which information is displayed. (2) In computer graphics, a predetermined part of a virtual space.

**Windows NT Operating System:** A multiuser, multitasking portable operating system designed by Microsoft for high end PC's used a servers.

**Word Processing:** Entering, editing and formatting text with the use of spelling checkers, outlining, tables, footnotes, and tables of contents. Synonym for text processing.

**Word Processor:** A computer programme which facilitates the creation of well formulated neat looking reports.

**Word:** A character string or a bit string treated as a unit for a given purpose. The length of a computer word is defined by the computer architecture, while the words in text processing are delimited by special characters or control characters.

**Workstation:** A functional unit that usually has special purpose computing capabilities and includes user-oriented input units and output units. Examples are a programmable terminal or a stand alone microcomputer.

**World Wide Web:** Each computer in the internet which can be referenced by a hypertext link is called a web page. A collection of web pages is known as the world wide web.

**WORM Optical disk:** An optical disk in which data is recorded in an irreversible manner such that, once written, it can be read many times and be appended on the remaining part of the recording surface, but not erased. WORM optical disk is the abbreviation for write once read multiple times optical disk.

**Worm:** A self-contained programme that can propagate itself through data processing systems or networks. Worms are often designed to use up available resources such as storage or processing time.

**Write Access**: An access right that gives permission to write data. Write access may grant permission to append, modify, delete, or create data.

**Write Ring**: A removable plastic or metal ring, the presence or absence of which on a magnetic tape reel prevents writing on the magnetic tape and thereby prevents the accidental erasure of a file. Synonymous with safety ring.

**Write-many**: Pertaining to a technique whereby a medium can be erased and written as many items as the physical medium allows.

**WYSIWYG:** Pertaining to a capability of a text processor or desktop publishing package to continually display pages or parts of pages as they will be printed. WYSIWYG display provides a constant display whereas print preview is a function that must be requested by the user. WYSIWYG is the abbreviation for what-you-see-is-what-you-get.

## X

**XML (Extensible Markup Language):** A widely used system for defining data formats. XML provides a very rich system to define complex documents and data structures such as invoices, molecular data, news feeds, glossaries, inventory descriptions, real estate properties, etc.

# Z

**Zero:** In data processing, the number that when added to or subtracted from any other number does not alter the value of that other number. Zero may have different representations in computers such as positively or negatively signed zero and floating-point-zero (in which the fixed-point part is zero while the exponent in the floating-point representation may vary).

**Zero suppression:** (1) The elimination of non-significant zeros from a numeral. (2) The function that allows the process by which unwanted zeros are omitted from the printed or displayed result in a calculation.

# SOME IMPORTANT QUESTIONS

## VOLUME-II

1. Define the following:
   (a) MIS (Management Information System)
   (b) Planning
   (c) Staffing
2. What do you mean by:
   (a) Authority
   (b) Contingency theory of leadership
   (c) *Laissez-faire* leadership
   (d) Motivation
3. Define:
   (a) Library system (b) Flow chart
4. What is meant by the term "operations research"?
5. Define the following keywords/terms:
   (a) Evaluation
   (b) TQM (Total Quality Management)
   (c) Scientific Management
   (d) Budget
   (e) Flexible Budget
6. Write in brief about the following terms:
   (a) Output device (b) Window
   (c) Unix (d) DBMS
   (e) Information Technology
   (f) Programming language

7. What is Telephone Network?
8. Write in 30-50 words on the following:
   (a) Packet switching (b) LAN
   (c) WAN (d) MAN
   (e) Ring Topology (f) ISDN
9. Explain the following terms in brief:
   (a) Fibre optics (b) Satellite Network
   (c) Apperture Cards (d) Chips
   (e) Microfitch
10. What is reflex copying (Negative/Positive)?
11. List different types of microforms
12. What are the following:
   (a) COM (Computer Output Microfilm)
   (b) Halftone illustrations
   (c) Silk screen printing
   (d) Intaglio printing
   (e) Desk Top Publishing
   (f) Screen Printing
   (g) Library Automation
13. Write in brief about:
   (a) Unimarc (b) CCF
   (c) CAS (d) SDI
   (e) Boolean Searches (f) Annotation
14. What is database approach?
15. Write in brief the levels of database architecture.
16. What is database schema?
17. What is artificial intelligence?
18. Explain the following terms:
   (a) Expert system (b) Operating system
   (c) Inter library loan (d) Acquisition
   (e) Document delivery service

19. How does telecommunication help in the exchange of information?
20. Write about the following items in 30-50 words each:
    (a) Message Switching Networks
    (b) Videotex
    (c) Electronic mail
    (d) Electronic journals
    (e) Video conferencing
    (f) BITNET
    (g) JANET
    (h) ASTINFO
21. Explain the automation facilities provided by Delnet?
22. What is NIC MAIL?
23. Write a few lines on the use of OPAC?
24. Enumerate five parts of communication process of Shanon.
25. What is the need of information centres?
26. Enumerate the different types of information centres.
27. Write 10 lines on National Documentation Centre.
28. Write in brief, on the following:
    (a) Special library
    (b) Data generation
    (c) Data dissemination
    (d) Data Bank
    (e) Data Centre
    (f) Data Referral Centre
    (g) CODATA
29. Explain the following terms:
    (a) Consideration of information
    (b) Information Analysis Centre
    (c) Research reports
    (d) Thesis
    (e) Patents
    (f) Citation Index
    (g) Trade Catalogue

30. Write 20 lines on Document Delivery Centre in India.
31. How in translation different from transliteration?
32. Define the following:
    (a) House Journal
    (b) Newsletter
    (c) Trade and Product Bulletin
    (d) Pamphlet
    (e) State-of-Art Report
    (f) Information Products
33. What are the important barriers to the use of information?
34. Discuss basic objectives of information consolidation.
35. What is trend report?
36. What do you understand by Technical Digest?
37. Describe the following terms:
    (a) Database (b) Gateway
    (c) Online (d) Terminal
    (e) Editors as intermediary (f) End user
    (g) Vendor (h) Database producer
38. What is Database Marketing?
39. Explain in brief how database intermediaries are of great help to end users?
40. What is online Retrieval System?
41. Explain two important advantages of Information Network.
42. What do you mean by standardization in information processing?
43. Which type of data are included in bibliographical databases?
44. What are the components of machine format?

45. Describe in brief the following:
    (a) UNISIST Reference Manual
    (b) ISO-2709
    (c) UK-MARC
    (d) US-MARC
    (e) Downloading
46. What is the purpose of CCF?
47. Write in brief the search processes involved in identifying relevant information?
48. How does UDC differ from DDC?
49. What are the major characteristics of LCC (Library of Congress Classification)?
50. What are the special characteristics of BC (Bibliographical Classification)?
51. Write in 30-50 words the trend of research in general classification systems?
52. Write in short on the following:
    (a) Common Isolates (b) Enumerative classification
    (c) Faceted classification (d) Hospitality in notation
    (e) Bibliometrics (f) Micro-opaque
    (g) Scientometrics (h) Keyword indexing
    (i) Database matching system
    (j) User friendly
53. Who are the original members of CRG?
54. Name the Indian Classificationist who has developed depth classification?
55. What is thesaurus? Mention its uses.
56. Mention the role of thesaurus in ISIR (Information Storage and Retrieval System)
57. List some of the important ISO standards for abbreviations.

58. Describe important recommendations of Paris Conference, 1961.
59. Discuss advantages of Past Controlled Vocabulary System?
60. What is ISAR (Information Storage and Retrieval System)?
61. What are the principle issues of ISAR compatibility?
62. List the five types of data suggested by Chen's model of search engine?
63. Explain the following terms:
    (a) Heuristic searching
    (b) Blackboard Architect
    (c) Search Strategy
    (d) Social epistechnology
    (e) Information professional
64. What is KGEU (Knowledge, Generation, Exchange and Utilisation)?
65. What constitutes 'Scientific Spirit'?
66. Define learning process and verbal learning?
67. Write in brief why "Library is a Learning Centre"?
68. Give reasons for considering IT as a tool of change?
69. Define the following keywords:
    (a) Information industry
    (b) Information Technology
    (c) View data
    (d) Information society
    (e) Information professionals
    (f) Hyper card
    (g) Mency
70. Distinguish between Information Economics and Economics of Information?
71. Explain the need of information policy?

72. Enumerate sources other than documentary sources, which constitute a National Information Policy?
73. Explain briefly the concept of "Multimedia"?
74. Distinguish between two terms 'Hypermedia' and 'Hypertext'?
75. Describe the advantages of CD-ROM technology?
76. Mention the important services provided by:
    (a) Indira Gandhi National Centre for Arts
    (b) Lalit Kala Academy
    (c) Sahitya Academy
    (d) ICSSR
    (e) ICHR
    (f) Nehru Memorial Museum and Library
77. Discuss how items of information are arranged in DEVSIS database?
78. Write brief notes on the following:
    (a) NASSIC, Baroda
    (b) Abstracting Service
    (c) Indexing Service
    (d) Secondary publications
79. What is the most significant difference between NISCAIR and DESIDOC?
80. Which centre is called the Indian MEDLARS centre?
81. Define Non-Disciplinary Information Sources?
82. Briefly mention the broad objectives of IFLA?
83. What do you mean by 'content analysis'?
84. Define 'Impact factor' in Citation Analysis?
85. What do yon mean by 'Aids to Information Sources'?
86. Discuss the role of librarian as an 'aid to Information Sources'?

87. Define the following terms:
    (a) Table of contents
    (b) Information personnel
    (c) Archivist
    (d) Linotype
    (e) WORM
    (f) Information Broker
    (g) Database Manager
88. Define Multimedia?
89. What is library authority?
90. Define the term 'cost effectiveness'?
91. Explain the main objectives of Resource Sharing?
92. What is INFLIBNET project, explain its objectives?
93. What is Local Library Network?